Strategies for Writing Success

by Kim Mitchell

illustrated by Linda Pierce

cover by Jeff Van Kanegan

photo credit: Digital Stock Corp.

Publisher
Instructional Fair • TS Denison
Grand Rapids, Michigan 49544

Instructional Fair • TS Denison grants the individual purchaser permission to reproduce patterns and student activity materials in this book for noncommercial individual or classroom use only. Reproduction for an entire school or school system is strictly prohibited. No other part of this publication may be reproduced in whole or in part. No part of this publication may be reproduced for storage in a retrieval system, or transmitted in any form or by any means, electronic, mechanical, recording, or otherwise, without the prior written permission of the publisher. For information regarding permission, write to Instructional Fair • TS Denison, P.O. Box 1650, Grand Rapids, MI 49501.

ISBN: 1-56822-962-3
Strategies for Writing Success
Copyright © 2000 by Instructional Fair Group
a Tribune Education Company
3195 Wilson Dr. NW
Grand Rapids, Michigan 49544

All Rights Reserved • Printed in the USA

Table of Contents

Chapter One: Beginnings: Searching for Ideas
Teacher Information 1
To the Student 4
Look and Listen 6
" . . . And That's Part of Our World Tonight" 8
"Extra! Extra!" 10
Stay Tuned 12
Who Is That Person? 13
You and Only You 14
Narrative and Reflective Papers 15
Creative Writing Assignments 16
The Teachers' Lounge 17

Chapter Two: Prewriting: Peer Discussion
Teacher Information 18
What Does That Word Mean? 22
Kind and Courteous, Please! 23
All for One and One for All! 25
Brainstorming and Free-Idea Exploration......27
We Are Alike and Different, Too 31
Practice Makes Perfect....................................32
Autobiographies/Biographies 33
This Is First and This Is Next 34
Narrative and Reflective Writing 35
Creative Writing 36
The Teachers' Lounge 38

Chapter Three: Prewriting: Mapping
Teacher Information 39
Example—Reports..42
Practice—Reports 43
Example—Persuasive 44
Practice—Persuasive 45
Example—Compare/Contrast 46
Practice—Compare/Contrast..........................47
Example—Autobiography/Biography 48
Practice—Autobiography/ Biography 49
Example/Practice—Process 50
Example—Creative Writing 51
Practice—Creative Writing.............................52
The Teachers' Lounge 53

Chapter Four: Prewriting: Listing and Outlining
Teacher Information 55
Report 57
Persuasive Paper 59
Compare/Contrast 61
Autobiography and Biography 63
Narrative, Reflective, and Process Papers......64
Creative Writing 67
Outlining 69
The Teachers' Lounge 73

Chapter Five: Drafting: Framing and First Drafts
Teacher Information 74
To the Student 76
Framing Focus..77
Rough Draft Construction 84
Rough Draft First Steps 85
Rough Draft—The Whole Package 86
The Teachers' Lounge 87

Chapter Six: Writing Process: Rewriting/Editing/Publishing
Teacher Information 88
Editing 89
Polishing for Perfection 90
Polishing and Publishing 91
The Teachers' Lounge 92

Introduction

The ability to write well is rarely based on raw talent. Like anything of value, learning to write well requires instruction, exploration, observation, practice, and commitment. Time-consuming, frustrating, and challenging, the art of writing well is worth the labor of learning it.

Writing, like speaking, is pivotal to good communication—no matter what the occupational or vocational goals. Once the writer has mastered the mechanics of writing clearly, the writer will have control over all types of communication. Those possibilities include expressing ideas on paper, establishing a point of view, exploring a theory, reflecting upon an experience or feeling, recording an event of merit, narrating a moment of sadness or happiness, or simply expanding a dream into a vivid story.

Learning to approach writing as a process will help remove the anxiety many students feel when assigned the task of writing a paper. Easy to learn, the writing process will build confidence rather than fear when students are asked to respond to an idea in writing.

This book will teach students a practical writing process for composing written assignments and help them to become good writers. It is not necessary to follow this book in a sequential order, as the chapters can be used individually to match the needs of students. However, if you are planning on developing a full understanding of writing strategies for different types of writing, then it may be beneficial to follow a chapter-by-chapter approach.

Each chapter contains an explanation of the section to be covered. The teacher's page will help you to best approach the learning activities provided for students. It helps you to prepare students and to assign any outside work that will be necessary to improve their understanding of the concepts and strategies.

Teaching writing strategies to students is a challenging and awesome task, but it has its rewards and is worth the effort. Students will become more confident as their skills improve and they master the art of the writing process.

CHAPTER ONE
Beginnings
Searching for Ideas

TEACHER INFORMATION

The writing process begins fairly easily. It encourages students to begin to understand their ability to gather and organize ideas for assessment for writing projects. As the teacher, you will be able to guide them through this first writing process step of idea selection and storage. The habit of gleaning ideas from daily life will help students to think and to assess what is viable and what is mundane. The writing process will help them to gain material for future tasks.

Students will benefit from learning to collect ideas from a variety of sources. They need to understand that to become good writers they need to assess the ideas they have about any given topic or assignment. They have to become familiar with what is happening in the world. They need to practice collecting ideas and staying aware of things around them. Most middle school students need help in understanding that ideas are everywhere and that developing the habit of paying attention to them will improve their writing.

This chapter will help students develop the habit of idea gathering. They will learn to be alert to things in the world that can be used for future writing topics. The activities and examples provided will offer them practice and build their confidence in understanding which ideas to collect and how to enhance them into more than a one-sentence idea. With practice and repetition of some of these tasks, they should be confident to start writing a paper.

One thing that will help students is to ask them to use a spiral notebook so they can record ideas. This *idea journal* will help them remember the events unfolding around them. They will want to form the habit of recording what they hear from the news, such as the details of the event and their reaction to what happened. Once recorded, they will have some topics they can discuss with their family members for further expansion of ideas. They can write about and expand these topics into written expressions of their ideas.

When you assign a class paper, students can refer to their idea journals and find topics to use. The biggest challenge for writing their papers will not be finding topics, because they will have collected several ideas from everything around them.

The more comfortable they are with finding ideas, the more willing students will be to start the process of writing a composition or an essay or a report. It is worth their time and effort to learn the process of being idea-prepared.

The activities in this chapter provide opportunities for students to practice gathering ideas using the beginning of the writing process approach. Each section addresses a specific way to gather ideas, depending on the type of writing task. The purpose of this idea gathering is to help students understand what they know about a given topic and empower them to search to learn more. The more they know about a topic, the more ideas they will have to develop a composition or writing assignment.

Each section is titled to identify the task and can be used according to the needs of skill mastery. Students will learn that they are responsible for learning about their world and for forming opinions and exploring ideas about the events that are shaping their lives and the lives of other people around the globe. With practice, students will learn that selecting key ideas for use in a quality composition is like picking jewels from the coal. They will learn to make good, intelligent choices regarding what ideas will enhance their assignments.

Look and Listen: This activity will help students gain confidence in understanding what they actually know now. Typically, middle school students have opinions, but they lack the confidence to express them in a writing assignment. This activity helps them to understand that they know more than they realize, and it helps them to begin the process of staying alert to ideas around them.

" . . . And That's Part of Our World Tonight" : This activity combines gleaning ideas, improving concentration skills, and taking notes from a source other than a textbook or chalkboard. This activity is a homework task, but it can be used in a classroom if students need practice taking notes from a television program. Using a video tape of the previous night's newscast may help students understand how to approach this task. Doing it one time in class may prove beneficial for students. After doing the assignment together, they will be ready to try it at home.

"Extra! Extra!": This activity can be done at home or in the classroom. Once again, it provides an opportunity for students to explore new ideas for writing papers and practice in note-taking skills.

"Stay Tuned!" Listening skills are the focus of this assignment. While students listen for more ideas from the news in their neighborhood, state, nation, and world, they will be able to practice focused listening and note taking.

Who Is That Person?: Providing exposure to resource material and expanding the idea that information is everywhere for the taking, this activity will help students work with encyclopedias, resource books and the Internet, if it is available.

You and Only You: The autobiography activity helps students to generate ideas for their papers by helping them to assess what they know about their own history. It also helps them to realize that they need to gain more information about their lives by interviewing family members and researching other reliable sources. They will better understand their personal history once they complete this task and write an autobiography.

Narrative and Reflective Papers: This activity moves students to the conceptual part of idea searching. Now they must think about their response to an idea they read about or listened to on the news. More inferential by design, this activity will help them understand their own impressions about ideas they have gleaned from a variety of sources.

Creative Writing Assignments: Students will enjoy having the opportunity to examine where they want to go with a creative writing short story before they actually begin writing. It is very easy to become lost in the building of the creative assignment. However, with this task, students will learn that the writing process helps them control and direct the events, the characters, and the structure of the plot.

The writing process will help students seek, retrieve, and understand their ideas. They will have more detail to build stronger main body paragraphs and expand their topics. This first step of the writing process, regardless of the type of writing assignment, will make them stronger and more enthusiastic writers.

To the Student

The assignments you are about to receive will teach you to use the writing process. The writing process is a method that will help you to organize from your first idea about a writing topic to its completed development and final copy composition. Also, this book will help you to understand how to use the writing process when working with the different types of writing that your teacher may assign. The more you experiment with different writing styles using the writing process, the more developed your writing style and writing confidence will become. Practice and experimentation in writing will make you more skilled. Relying on the structure of the writing process will give you the confidence to try.

The terms listed below will help you to understand some of the styles of writing that are available. Scan the list of terms now and return to the terms list if you do not understand a type of writing as you complete the various assignments.

Writing is an exciting way to learn about the world around you. When you take the time to practice the writing process with different writing tasks, you will have a good, dependable writing approach that will help you to develop the best possible finished assignment. Any type of writing assignment will be improved through the writing process. You will learn how to make the most of your ideas, the structure, your actual writing, and the polishing of the paper you are writing.

The **writing process** is a way to approach writing assignments that helps you to develop logical, well-developed compositions. It helps you to organize the way you approach the task of putting your ideas on paper and then organizing those ideas so that they make sense. It is a method that will keep you in control of any writing assignment. The steps for the writing process include idea searching, prewriting, developing rough drafts, scrutinizing your first attempts, revising and revising, editing and revising again, and polishing copy.

Like an essay, a **report** is a paper that details facts about a particular place, person, or event. This paper is used primarily for a social studies class, a science class, or an English class. An essay and report can be similar in structure and details. A report means that you need to do your background work and know what you are discussing in your paper. Encyclopedias, other resource books, and the Internet can help you to learn about your subject so you can write with authority. Completing reports will become a comfortable writing style for you to use in middle school, high school, college, and even in the work place when you are older.

An **autobiography** is a story about you. Details about your background, interesting anecdotes or stories, and interesting experiences are included in an autobiography.

Although a **biography** is similar to an autobiography, it is different because it is about another person, not about you. A biography can detail the same things that an autobiography does.

A **persuasive paper** is one that encourages a particular opinion or view. This kind of writing is used in most classes in which you are expected to have an opinion with supporting detail to develop that opinion. It requires that you know your material, so it is important to learn as much as possible about the subject being developed in a persuasive paper.

Comparison and/or contrast is a good writing style to use when you want to explain similarities and differences between people or things. If you want to write about how authors were very similar or very different or both, or how two organisms lead mirror lives, or how governments during World War II were the same or dramatically opposite in their approach to the war, this is the type of writing for that assignment.

Narrative writing includes descriptive details or anecdotes (interesting details). A narrative is an interesting way of adding details and description to a variety of different styles of writing.

Reflective writing involves writing about thoughts, reactions, or insight you have gained from observing a historical event, a current issue, a theme in a novel, an experience, the mood of a poem, or a variety of other situations.

Process writing details a function or a routine. It may explain the process of a task, a procedure, or a function.

Creative writing can be a short story or a number of other creative projects that benefit from following the writing process structure.

It does not matter what the writing task may be, the writing process is the key to controlling and developing a writing assignment to achieve the best possible results. The writing process will help you develop your writing potential and ability.

Idea Searching

Name _____

Look and Listen

Writing a paper about a subject you know very little about is a difficult and frustrating task. It is challenging to organize a paper, but if you have no knowledge or very little knowledge of a topic, it becomes almost overwhelming. However, this situation can be remedied very easily. It only requires that you begin to collect ideas and develop a good base of things you *do* know.

Your life is filled with information. You can find out about all sorts of things from what is going on around you in your city or town to what is happening halfway around the globe. All you have to do is find out what you know now, take a good look at what you would like to know, and then start to look and listen to what is happening. Once you become comfortable with really observing things, you will begin to learn more about people, society, and the world. The more you know, the more you can express in a paper that will now have supporting information to make your writing believable.

A good place to start is listing what you do know now. Consider what is happening in the political arena, the schools, the town, sports, and the news media. Jot down what you know to begin understanding how aware you are of the things that are happening in your world. From this first assessment you can decide how to be more tuned in to your world so you will have something to write about in future papers and compositions.

Directions: List what you know about current situations that are happening in each of the following:

Your neighborhood _____
_____

Your school _____
_____

Your local government _____
_____

Current news events _____
_____

Current sporting events/happenings _____
_____

The political scene in your country _____
_____

Idea Searching

Name _____

What is happening on a global scale? Explain what and where. _____
_____
_____
_____

Next, begin the process of actually paying attention to the areas you just considered so that you understand what you need to learn if you want to be a writer capable of adding depth to a composition. For a few days, look and listen and add new details to the same areas. Pay attention to how much you learn by just listening and asking questions. Remember, the more you know, the stronger your supporting information in a composition.

Directions: Add more information to the same areas that you worked with before. Compare your lists after you decided to look and listen to your world. Make an effort to become more alert to your changing world.

Your neighborhood _____
_____

Your school _____
_____

Your local government _____
_____

Current news events _____
_____

Current sporting events/happenings _____
_____

The political scene in your country _____
_____

What is happening on a global scale? Explain what and where. _____
_____

Any other area of interest _____
_____
_____

Idea Searching

Name _____

"...And That's Part of Our World Tonight"

As you continue to advance in middle school, you probably will be expected to write more papers than you have in previous classes. You are on the verge of becoming a young adult. Your teachers will expect you to think and to respond to the world around you by writing about the things you observe. Finding topics is always a bit of a challenge, so you will need to practice idea searching. Watching the news at night, reading the newspaper, and listening to the news on the radio will help you to develop ideas for writing.

Your world is filled with problems that need solutions, conditions that need change, and events that need praise. You have access to hundreds of ideas each day if you stay alert to the things happening around you. The following activity will help you learn the art of idea searching. Practice listening and recording your ideas.

Directions: Listen to a newscast on television tonight. Use this sheet to practice recording ideas that you get by listening to the program. Choose topics that you find interesting in the news part, the human interest sections (stories about people and their daily lives), or sports. Pay close attention, as details will be delivered fairly quickly by the news team.

Program name_____ Date _____
Topic of a news story _____
What happened? _____
Give the details. _____
_____

What is the result of this situation or problem, or has it been resolved yet? _____
_____
_____

What is your reaction to this situation?_____
_____
_____

Do some idea searching on a human interest story (about a real person and an event in his or her daily life). Who is the person? (If you missed the name, attempt to explain if it is a businessperson, a housewife, a teacher . . . .) _____
What is the story about?_____
_____
_____

© Instructional Fair • TS Denison

Idea Searching

Name _____

What is the problem or the success for this person? _____
_____

What has happened in this situation? Is the person satisfied with the outcome? _____
_____

What is your reaction to what happened to this person? _____
_____
_____

Idea search a sports event story (listen for unfair rulings in a game, a trade of a sports person to another team, a significant success by a player, team, coach, or fan).
What is the sports event? _____
_____

What are the details of this sports situation? _____
_____

What is the outcome of this situation or is it ongoing? _____
_____

What is your reaction to the situation you detailed? _____
_____
_____

Discuss what you observed with someone in your family. Perhaps a parent or guardian watched the same sportscast and has some ideas about those topics, too. Ask for opinions of the news stories you recorded. If this person did not watch the stories, then explain the details and ask his or her opinions. Record these opinions below so that you have another viewpoint of the same event. Noting this difference in opinion is an exciting way to begin to see that most situations have more than one side. Understanding those sides helps you to write an interesting paper if you decide to choose one of these topics.

Record a family member's opinion of the same news story below.
News story _____
_____
_____

Human interest story _____
_____
_____

Sports story _____
_____
_____

Idea Searching

Name _____

"Extra! Extra!"

Directions: Use a daily newspaper and do the following to continue to practice being alert to the world around you. Read carefully.

Your first article should be from the news section. It usually will be in the first section of the newspaper and will involve some problem with the government, crime, politics, the schools, or a global event. This type of article will help you to form opinions about life conditions that you may write about in essays, reports, comparison/contrast, and persuasion papers. Collect ideas like this whenever you pick up the newspaper. The more you learn about a particular news situation, the stronger your opinion will be when writing a paper about it.

From the news section, give the following information:
Newspaper _____
Date_____ Article title _____
Writer _____ Page of article _____
(If there is no particular writer's name, use the term Staff. If there is no byline which gives the writer's name, a staff member on the paper is writing the article.)
Who are the people involved in this story? _____
_____
What is the article about? _____
_____
What is the problem for the people involved? _____
_____
How is this problem going to be solved, or is it still a problem? _____
_____
What is your reaction to what happened to the people in this story? _____
_____
How do you think it should be solved? _____
_____

Now, choose an article from the feature section of the newspaper. The feature section of the newspaper may be found under different headings such as Feature or Life or Living, but it is the section that is about real people involved in real-life situations. Not as dramatic as the front section with the news articles, this section will offer stories about people dealing with illness, or a new business, or an invention, or an accomplishment that is very impressive. The feature section offers information helpful in writing biographies or reflective or narrative style papers.

Idea Searching

Name _____

Article title _____ Page _____
Writer's name _____ What caused you to choose this article?
_____
Who are the people involved in this story? _____
_____
What is the story about? _____
_____
What interesting details did you learn about this situation? _____
_____
What did you learn about people and the way they function or handle life? _____
_____
What is your reaction to this story? _____
_____
_____

Next, turn to the sports section of the newspaper. In this section you will find statistics and other interesting details about games and playoffs and other sporting events. But you will also find information about players, coaches, or teams and recent events that have happened to them. The sports section offers ideas about the rights of players, the poor treatment of a coach, or an unfair ruling against a team. Reading this section will help you to record ideas that you may use when writing biographies, persuasive papers, comparison/contrast papers, or process papers. Collecting ideas about events in this section will offer another direction for a paper.

Article title _____ Page _____
Writer's name _____ What caused you to choose this article?
_____
Who are the people involved in this story? _____
_____
What is the story about? _____
_____
List several important details about this event. _____
_____
What did you learn about fair treatment of a player, coach, or team? _____
_____
What is your reaction to this story? _____
_____
_____

© Instructional Fair • TS Denison

Idea Searching

Name _____

Stay Tuned

Directions: Learning about your world to help you have something to say when you write a paper is worth the effort it takes to pay attention to the events happening around you. Simply listening to the radio will provide you with information on most subjects. Like the newscast on television, you need to focus on what is being said, because it will be quickly delivered. Take notes as you ride in a car or as you listen to your radio elsewhere. Continue to build your idea file of things you do know about so that, when the time comes and you need to write about something, you can refer to a well-developed list of ideas. Plus, there is an added benefit of listening to the news on a radio; it helps you improve your listening skills.

What is happening in local news today? _____
_____
_____

What is happening in world news today? _____
_____
_____

What is happening in sports today? Listen for local, national, and global sports news.
_____
_____
_____

What story did you hear that you felt was unfair for the people involved? Explain what happened, to whom, and why it seemed unfair. _____
_____
_____

What news story would you like to learn more about? _____
_____
_____
_____
_____
_____

Idea Searching

Name _____

Who Is That Person?

The biography, which is about a person, has a different idea structure. Unlike the persuasive or general report, the biography requires some research from published sources like encyclopedias, resource books about people, or the Internet. Certainly, if you are writing a report about a significant person who is currently in the news, you could use a newscast, the newspaper, or radio. You know how to record detail from those sources from the assignments in this book. However, if you are writing a biography about a famous person who lived long ago, the following idea search will help you to record details in preparation for the next step in the writing process. Once you have your ideas logged, you will have information to begin discussing and organizing an outline for writing.

You have many sources to choose from when looking for details about a famous person. You must acknowledge your sources, so it is important to record each source and to accurately provide information about it. If it is an encyclopedia, then you need to fill in the blanks below. Be accurate and skim the resources to glean details that you feel will help you write a clear and detailed biography.

Directions: After you have determined the subject of your biography, then do the following. Select an encyclopedia and read an article about the person you have selected. Next, fill in the following areas.

Biography topic _____

Encyclopedia - Title, publisher, copyright date _____

_____

Volume and page number _____

Background details about the person (consider place of birth, date of birth, family details, education) _____

_____

_____

What else did you learn about the person? _____

_____

_____

_____

Idea Searching

Name _____

You and Only You

An autobiography is a paper about you. If you are using the writing process, you will want to follow the pattern of seeking ideas first to determine what you know about yourself. List details about yourself before you write so you can determine the depth of your paper. More than likely, you will need to find more information about yourself. You may have to ask a relative for anecdotes or interesting stories about your childhood. You may need to research some of the particular names of schools you attended when you were a little boy or girl. Using the writing process approach to gathering details will help you to determine how well you can develop your autobiography.

Directions: Fill in the following areas. You may have to return to this assignment several times if you need to ask a relative for help.

Date of birth and place of birth _____

Interesting information about your name _____
_____

Family information (brothers, sisters, parents, grandparents . . .) _____
_____
_____

A childhood memory to share _____
_____
_____

Schools attended _____
_____

A school memory _____
_____

What things have you done that have made you proud? _____
_____

What are some of your goals and plans? _____
_____

Remember, you want to jot down details from memory and from the input of family members. If you are adopted, you still have memories, as you are a member of the family you live with now. Record your memories and then assess what you need to add for more detail before you begin the next step in the writing process.

Idea Searching

Name _____

Narrative and Reflective Papers

Use the writing process to launch an idea search for both a narrative and a reflective paper. Narrative and reflective papers share a similar pattern because they tend to be more detailed and descriptive. The idea search will deal more with ideas than facts.

Directions: Fill in the idea search in preparation for writing your narrative paper.

Topic _____ The purpose for this narrative is _____

_____

List some of the ideas you would like to include in your paper. _____
_____
_____

What further information do you need to expand your ideas into a paper? _____
_____
_____

Using the writing process, do a similar idea search for a reflective paper.
What is the topic of this paper? _____
What is your purpose for this paper? _____
What ideas do you have for writing this paper? _____
_____
_____

What other ideas do you need to investigate to develop a strong paper? _____
_____
_____
_____

Using the writing process to discover what ideas you know and what ideas and details you still need to learn, you should be able to prepare for the next step of the writing process. When you have recorded ideas, investigated other ideas, and added to the ideas you know, then you will be in a position to discuss the potential topics with others in your class before you begin another step of brainstorming or mapping.

© Instructional Fair • TS Denison   15   IF19316 Strategies for Writing Success

Idea Searching

Name _____

Creative Writing Assignments

The search for ideas will improve any short story or creative writing assignment. You will want to list ideas about the characters you develop, the setting of the story, the conflicts the characters will face, or the actual plot. You need to list these ideas so that you know what you have to work with and what you need to continue to imagine. The more ideas you imagine before you discuss, brainstorm, and map it, the more control you will have when you begin to write your paper.

Directions: Record ideas as you imagine them in the areas listed below.

Story idea _____

Main character—who, what, description. Provide several details to provide depth for this imagined character. _____
_____
_____

Another character—provide the same type of detail (who, what, and description). _____
_____
_____

List other characters and their traits (details about them). _____
_____
_____

Where will this story take place? (Describe the setting carefully.) _____
_____
_____

Conflicts—what are some of the problems the characters will face? _____
_____
_____

Review what you have imagined. What will you tell someone your story is going to be about if they ask you? This will help you understand the plot of your story so you can maintain that focus once you move to the other writing process steps. _____
_____
_____

List any other ideas you might like to add to your story in this space. Use this sheet when you move through the writing process and produce the actual story. _____
_____
_____

Beginnings

THE TEACHERS' LOUNGE

From News to Writing Idea—The idea section of the writing process offers an opportunity to expose all students to current events. Using a bulletin board, display headlines of significant current events. You may offer students extra credit to investigate the events for the headlines and report to the class what is happening in each situation. Allotting a few minutes each class period for current events updates will help students become fairly well educated about what is happening in today's world.

Once a week it may be beneficial to expand the details of current events into a class discussion, demonstrating how to turn what is happening in the news into topics for writing compositions. Use the ideas you and your students have discussed from the options on the current events bulletin board. Choose a few of the current events that students have heard discussed so they know the situation. Expand those topics on the chalkboard where you can demonstrate how to transform details from a current event into a workable theory for writing a report, a persuasive paper, a comparison, or a contrast paper. A few chalkboard examples will help middle school students make the transition from fact to idea to writing project.

This Famous Person Wrote—Read quality nonfiction pieces to students to expose them to models for writing compositions. There are many nonfiction pieces of merit in most textbooks. Exposure to these will enhance awareness of style and structure. It is important to point out the topic of the nonfiction piece before you read it to students. Referring to that topic as you progress through the material will teach students how to stay focused when writing. Also, as each detail unfolds, it will help students understand how details are used in a composition to enhance the topic.

Read to students rather than encouraging a round-robin reading activity. You will have the opportunity to stop and teach from the material rather than stopping a student who may be struggling with the first reading of a sophisticated piece of writing. You can control the pace and the emphasis and demonstrate successful oral reading behavior.

Creative Writing Vocabulary Development—Find a section of a bulletin board and build a descriptive vocabulary wall. You may choose to put a trait or descriptive phrase on the chalkboard each day and have students take turns writing and designing it for bulletin board display. The words can be simple descriptive adjectives for detail about a person's appearance or they can be words describing personality and quirks. The outcome will be that students will learn new language and description for use in their creative writing tasks.

CHAPTER TWO
Prewriting
Peer Discussion

TEACHER INFORMATION

Prewriting is an important part of the writing process. Prior to prewriting, the writing student has been working with the idea searching portion of the process. The work they did in that area should help them to have a base of knowledge suitable for conversion into a composition or a creative-writing task. That first step of the writing process—the idea searching—is as important as this step, which involves discussion of ideas with peers or classmates.

Peer discussion means that once a decision is made on the type of paper students will be assigned, they have the opportunity to discuss ideas before they begin to write their papers. This interaction helps each student listen and learn from the ideas offered by classmates. Peer discussion helps students to see another side to the same topic or idea, and it helps them to make intellectual leaps regarding other angles of the same idea. Also, when there is peer discussion, students can assume the role of active participant with someone on their level rather than simply listening to the teacher expound on the topic or lead a class discussion. When you, the teacher, step back to coach the groups that are engaged in peer discussion, a different level of thinking interaction begins.

Peer discussion should have boundaries that are put into place before the activity begins. First, create groups of no more than three members. It is possible to have larger ones, but groups of three or even two provide a smaller, more manageable size, and usually all members of each group remain actively engaged in the discussion. There is a tendency with groups larger than three for a few students not to be heard, especially if they are quiet or shy.

Be alert to the dynamics of each group. If students are allowed to choose their own groups, the discussion and behavior of each group should be monitored. Some combinations of students will easily move off task if they feel you are not interested in their discussion. If you decide to create groups yourself, you can team students who, based on previous classroom behavior and performance, will work best together. Blending very successful students with students who need that extra nudge tends to be beneficial for everyone. Either way, the group dynamics should be considered as your students team for peer discussion.

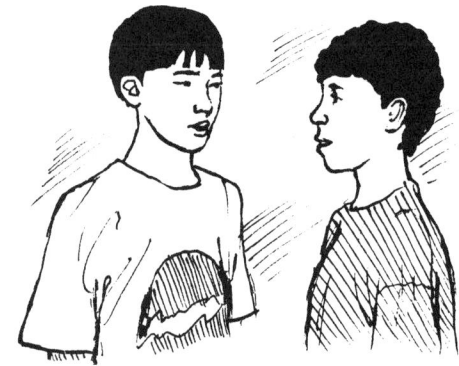

Encourage students to use the activities in this chapter to record and expand their ideas in preparation for writing. They may feel that they can remember all they discussed, but unless they record the information, they will lose a record of how their raw ideas became strong writing topics. You will also have a listing of their work.

One student in each group should be in charge of each task within the peer discussion. There are many formal ways to form groups, and your teacher intuition will probably be the best tool to use. You know your students, and you know what they can accomplish or what will frustrate them and slow their ability to be successful. If you rely on your own feelings about which student will be best in each peer discussion job, then group interactions will probably be successful.

One person should record the ideas. This student must quickly write ideas that are suggested and then expanded as the group discusses them. The best choice for this job is a student who is not intimidated by listening and writing quickly.

A second person should keep everyone on task. This person will be involved in the discussion but also will remind other students to stay on the topic and not drift or become distracted. Since this is a very diplomatic job, it is best to select a student who will not be rude or aggressive when nudging a peer to return to the topic.

A third student will shift the group to new ideas and topics. This student should observe when the group is ready to make that discussion shift. When it is obvious that the discussion of a current idea is reaching an end, this student will be in the position to offer a new idea for consideration.

All students in a team or peer discussion group will participate in the idea exploration. All have their own jobs to perform, but they are also free to discuss, explore, examine, and expand each topic in this prewriting part of the writing process.

You may have other good ideas for assigning jobs for the peer discussion activity. There really is no right or wrong way to have students work during peer discussion. The key is to encourage them to be actively engaged in the task of exploring an idea by peer interaction.

Prewriting is a valuable step in the writing process. It helps students to organize their thoughts and expand those thoughts into interesting writing topics. This part of the writing process also helps students learn to work as a team and to share ideas. It is a worthwhile classroom activity and important in teaching students to learn to think in preparation for writing.

Prewriting: Laying the Bricks for a Courteous Journey

One main issue in this chapter is to help students become good team members when they are working with other students. It takes time and practice to learn how to be a strong and positive team member when beginning the writing process. The sooner students learn that kindness and courtesy count as much as intellectual input, the more successful the teams will be. All students will benefit from the extra steps they take to learn how to make teams work well together.

Also, they will learn that the prewriting section of the writing process involves different brainstorming methods and that free-idea exploration is probably the most comfortable in form and restrictions. Students can explore how to use this free method of brainstorming an idea both with teams and alone. The practice exercises will help them to gain confidence in approaching prewriting and to understand that it is a valuable way to assess their own depth of knowledge of a topic. Rather than nurture the belief that the best way to write a paper is to do just that—write a paper—this chapter will help students to understand that spending time prewriting and using free-idea exploration will result in a well-written, detail-supported assignment. The result will be successful because students will have considered the paper's content before they began the rough draft.

Kind and Courteous, Please!: This activity will help students lay the groundwork for courteous team interaction. Without making it clear that courtesy is the only acceptable behavior, there will be problems. Students will benefit from rules that make certain that negative responses do not happen. They will learn that it is okay to disagree as long as that difference in opinion about the idea is not in the form of an attack on an individual. When students make their own rules, they will have a personal stake in the success of the outcome.

All for One and One for All!: Knowing what job belongs to whom will keep all students on task and functioning within the team. Some students are natural workers and like to take over as many jobs as possible. As much as that enthusiasm is envied, it also can overwhelm students who tend not to participate as frequently. Giving jobs to all students guarantees that they will all participate.

Brainstorming and Free-Idea Exploration: This activity will help students understand the concept of brainstorming and letting ideas flow. Unlike the more structured brainstorming approaches, this free-idea exploration format allows for recording ideas without regard to form. Students enjoy this method because of the freedom to write what is on their minds and to organize later. It helps them remember all the ideas before they begin the process of eliminating those that will not match their writing task. This section offers practice dealing with persuasive papers.

We Are Alike and Different, Too: This activity provides more practice in free exploration and will help students understand how to brainstorm for comparison and/or contrast papers.

Autobiographies/Biographies: Practice in writing the free-idea exploration for autobiographies and biographies is offered in this section. Autobiographies and biographies are similar in structure, so this brainstorming task will help develop ideas for either assignment.

This Is First and This Is Next . . . : This method of brainstorming lends itself well to process writing, since process writing is so orderly and structured. Students tend to be comfortable using this brainstorm method for process papers.

Narrative and Reflective Writing: Narrative and reflective papers require students to have some base of knowledge that they will react to and write about in an assignment. This section helps students brainstorm what they may want to include in that paper. The free-idea exploration brainstorm is a good method for students to use to understand their knowledge of a given topic. If they are unable to expand in this form of brainstorming, they will understand that they need more background work before they are prepared to complete this step.

Creative Writing: It is fun to brainstorm in free-idea exploration style when organizing for a creative writing assignment. Students love to write short stories, so the ability to generate ideas about a main character, minor characters, plot, and setting through brainstorming is one they enjoy. This task will help them think through a creative idea to a more defined story possibility.

What Does That Word Mean?

The following vocabulary words will be used in this chapter. You may know some of them and others may be new to you. If you struggle with a vocabulary word in one of the activity sections or you need more help understanding a concept that is presented, return to this page and review the word that is causing the confusion. The words are presented in the order in which they are used in the chapters.

prewriting—to organize and plan before actually writing a composition or report or creative assignment. This is part of the writing process, and it helps you explore ideas, expand other ideas, and find details to be used in your paper. Prewriting is necessary, as it will help you create a strong and well-developed writing assignment.

purpose—what is the reason for writing a particular paper? Determining your purpose will give direction to your writing and help you stay focused while you write. A purpose is similar to a compass; it will guide you in structuring your paper.

peer—a person of equal status or standing. A peer is a classmate or someone in the same social level or a similar situation as you.

sequence—a series that follows in a step-by-step order. It has a continuous pattern to it.

brainstorming—a process of allowing ideas to flow freely in order to expand thinking. These ideas are sometimes hurried and resemble a "storm" in that they may be spontaneous and without order, but they have depth and are worthwhile.

mapping—organizing ideas in a pattern that "maps" or "webs" ideas by linking one to the other. When finished, the idea linking resembles a creative pattern of ideas. This is a prewriting activity to help expand ideas before writing a composition.

outline—a more formal structure and listing of ideas in a prewriting situation. Outlining helps form a pattern of how to write a composition.

framing—to imagine how you want your composition or report or creative assignment to be structured. Framing helps you to consider what you need to state in your introductory paragraph, how you will develop and expand your main body, and how you will approach your conclusion to be effective and complete your idea.

Peer Discussion

Name _____

Kind and Courteous, Please!

This part of the writing process will allow you and your classmates to work in teams to discuss those ideas you have been gathering in your idea journal or for the assignments in the last chapter. This is the time for you to discuss your ideas with a few other students in your class, your peers. Working together, you will expand some of the ideas all of you have been collecting with the purpose of eventually developing a few of those ideas in a composition. Teamwork is the key to this activity, so it is important to work courteously in this group.

When you work in a team, respect one another's opinions. Just as you may take an unusual or creative direction in this part of the writing process, so may your peers. If you all plan on following the rules for a civil discussion, your participation in a team will be a rewarding one.

Directions: Before you begin the peer discussion, list what you feel to be necessary to create a positive environment for teamwork. List those ideas below with brief explanations and be prepared to discuss them with the whole class. Your teacher will then help you and your classmates develop the basic rules for peer discussion that will be followed by everyone in your classroom. Discuss the following areas and devise solutions to each situation. If you do not understand some of the ideas listed below, ask your teacher to explain them to your team.

Rules for Peer Discussion
1. Taking turns _____
2. Listening _____
3. Asking questions _____
4. Joining in _____
5. Interrupting _____
6. Politely disagreeing _____
7. Majority rules? _____
8. Your fair share _____
9. Freedom from criticism _____
10. (your choice) _____

Your list may look like this when you are finished.

1. Taking turns - wait until a person is finished speaking before adding your ideas.
   Rule: Wait your turn.

2. Listening behavior - pay attention to what is being said, do not tap on the desk, look away, or doodle.
   Rule: Pay attention to each other.

3. Asking questions - ask questions that add to the discussion, think about what you want to ask rather than wasting time asking questions that are not related to the discussion.
   Rule: Think before you ask.

4. Joining in - be part of the group, do not just sit there.
   Rule: Participate.

5. Interrupting - do not just blurt out information while someone else is talking.
   Rule: Do not interrupt.

6. Politely disagreeing - no name calling, no personal attacks, or angry displays if you disagree with an individual or the team.
   Rule: Be polite at all times.

7. Majority rules? - if one person disagrees in the group, then we will vote.
   Rule: Be fair.

8. Your fair share - everyone is a member of the team, everyone has a job, everyone must participate.
   Rule: All have a job to do.

9. Freedom from criticism - we will approach unique ideas as unique, not bad.
   Rule: Freedom to think differently is allowed.

10. (your choice) - (this will be decided by your group)
    Rule: This will be decided by your group.

Place the rules on a sheet of construction paper for display in the classroom. Not only will you follow the rules you designed in your group, you will also respect the rules designed by other groups in your classroom. These rules will help you enjoy this part of the writing process free of negative reactions by anyone in your team.

Peer Discussion

All for One and One for All!

A peer is someone who is your equal. Your teacher is not your peer; however, other teachers are peers to your teacher. Your peers are the other students in your classroom. When you become a team with other classmates and begin to have peer discussion, you are on equal footing. You will need to designate who does what, and all members of your team will be responsible to share ideas, respect what others are saying, and fulfill their part of the team's assignment.

You will be expected to explore an idea for the type of paper your teacher assigns. Each member of your team will be expected to do something that will help the discussion move smoothly.

One member of your team will record, or write down, ideas as you discuss them. This person must be quick at putting ideas down on paper, able to listen carefully to what other team members are saying, and able to add to the discussion. It is a challenging job, because it is important for the next steps in the writing process.

A second person in the team will be responsible for keeping the team on task. This person must be alert to changes in attitude and attention. It is easy to drift away from the assignment and begin to socialize. That is when this person will nudge the group back to the assignment. Ideas will flow better when everyone is fully committed to the assignment. This team member needs to be diplomatic and not hostile when he or she requests a team member or the whole group to return to the assignment.

Another person will suggest new ideas once discussion slows down or hits a "brick wall." This task requires "thinking on your feet" (thinking quickly and adding suggestions).

Peer Discussion

Name _____

Directions: Now that your teammates have an understanding of who is to do what job, fill out the following and begin brainstorming on a topic related to your school's policies. This is a practice assignment, so the topic will be easier if it is something everyone in your group has some knowledge about. Perhaps the topic you choose will be the tardy policy of the school, the amount of time for lunch, or the rules about the dress code. Choose something that has a bit of controversy or potential for argument. This will be your team's first attempt at working together as a group. Everyone should have an assigned job and practice a courteous and polite way of working as a group. Also, it is important to notice successes and problems as you work together. This is a learning attempt, so be honest when you evaluate what you did as a team.

Name of the person recording detail _____

Name of the person keeping the team on the topic _____

Name of the person suggesting other ideas _____

What was the topic your group discussed? _____

What did you learn about this topic during your team discussion? _____

_____

_____

In what areas did team members agree? _____

_____

_____

In what areas did team members disagree? _____

_____

_____

What could be improved for more success as a team, and how could that be accomplished?

_____

_____

What new rules for team interaction would help a team work more effectively? _____

_____

_____

Peer Discussion

Brainstorming and Free-Idea Exploration

A first step in the prewriting phase of the writing process is to expand ideas from the idea search collection to the prewriting exploration of that idea. This is accomplished in a step that is called *brainstorming*. Brainstorming involves allowing your brain, or your thinking, to almost swirl and churn until new ideas are found. Those ideas are recorded on paper and stored for further use as you move to the actual writing stage of the writing process. However, brainstorming is such a successful method that it is worth enjoying in several activities in this chapter.

Brainstorming can follow a method known as *free-idea exploration*, which means that you simply list the ideas and their compatible details as they relate to the topic you are going to explore in a composition. There are many methods of brainstorming. We will explore the process of brainstorming in free-form method.

The form for free-idea exploration brainstorming varies depending on the type of composition, report, or paper you are planning to write. The basic approach of brainstorming and letting ideas flow remains the same, but how you put the ideas on paper changes a little with each paper you want to write.

Just as you change equipment when you change sports—so it is true with free-idea exploration. When you write a serious, formal paper like a persuasive paper, a comparison and/or contrast paper, or a report, it will help you to have a stronger understanding of your paper if you look at both sides of the topic. Whether you agree with both sides is not the point. Understanding that there is another way of looking at the same subject will give your paper more depth of detail.

Imagine that the topic you are going to write about deals with a rule at your school. Perhaps you want to write a persuasive paper, one that persuades people to disagree with the rule and encourage changing it. Imagine that the rule is no hats in class. This is a rule you are not fond of because you enjoy wearing a baseball cap, as do your male and female friends. After you have thought about it and casually discussed it with your friends, you now have an even stronger belief that the rule of no hats in the classroom should be changed.

© Instructional Fair • TS Denison

IF19316 Strategies for Writing Success

The ideal way to brainstorm is to start with a sheet of paper and invite a few of your peers (classmates) to discuss the idea you think might become a good paper. As you talk it over and consider the angles, try to look at both the positive and negative sides of the rule or law. This two-sided method of observation will keep you from developing a paper that is just emotional and argumentative. When you consider both sides of any topic, you will have a logical paper showing that you considered the reasons for the rule and still feel that it needs changing. Your overall paper will reflect careful consideration of all viewpoints.

Also, when you brainstorm with your peers about a particular issue for a persuasive paper, you may discover that the idea you were considering really is not strong enough for a full composition. This will help you avoid partially completing the paper and then deciding that it just will not work. You will not waste your time. Plus, rather than eliminate an idea that is not strong enough for a full paper, you may want to save that idea and use it another time as you gain more information about that topic from reading newspaper articles or watching the news on television. Like seeds in a garden, each idea has the potential to become a good paper if it is nurtured. An idea you do not use today may become an excellent paper later after you nurture it with more knowledge.

Once you begin to discuss an idea with your peers, jot down the ideas as they develop. Since this is a free-idea exploration brainstorm, note ideas as they strike you as interesting or worthwhile.

For example, a free-idea exploration on the subject of hats in school may look like the following:

Subject—hats in school

Side One—Reasons for a hat rule:
impolite/contrary to courtesy . . . rude to wear a hat in a building . . . teachers cannot see your face with a low brim . . . can be used to identify with a particular group . . . is a distraction to learning . . . rules are rules

Side Two—Reasons for eliminating a hat rule:
you can still be courteous with a hat on . . . famous people wear hats all the time . . . the brim can be raised in the classroom . . . it is a fashion statement . . . individuality

This listing of ideas could be the beginning of more involved brainstorming. It would help you to get a feeling about the potential for writing this paper.

Peer Discussion

Name _____

When you have finished with simply listing ideas in free-idea exploration, you can make the next leap and decide what might work for a paper direction. For example, you would review the material about hats that you just developed to see where the logical direction would be regarding the ideas on the brainstorm sheet. Your next step would be to write possible persuasive approaches that might work for developing a strong paper.

Paper direction: Removing hats supports the tradition of respect or rules and polite behavior. This paper could follow that idea and persuade people to respect a no-hat rule.

Or you could approach the paper from a different direction:

Paper direction: Eliminating the hat rule in the classroom allows for freedom of choice.

Either direction has potential for a paper based on the ideas you brainstormed in that writing process step, so it would be your decision to make the choice based on what you know and what you believe. When you can make a commitment to a paper based on knowledge and research, you will surely develop a good paper.

Now it is your turn to try this free-idea exploration style of brainstorming using a topic you are interested in. Do the following and remember to approach each side of the issue fairly.

Directions: To practice this free-idea exploration, first try a subject on your own and just jot down ideas as they develop. Once you decide on a subject, remember to write ideas from both sides of the subject to develop a fair and accurate view. Ideas do not have to be written in complete sentences.

Free-idea exploration: your topic choice (choose a topic to persuade or prove something)

Subject _____ persuasive direction you are interested in developing (What would you want to persuade people to consider?) _____
_____

One view of the subject _____
1. _____
2. _____
3. _____
4. _____

Peer Discussion

Name _____

An opposite view of the subject _____
1. _____
2. _____
3. _____
4. _____

Working with a few peers, develop the same subject, combining their ideas to develop the two views of the same subject. This will help you understand how other people think about the subject you just investigated on your own, and it may help you to nurture new ideas about the same subject. Also, remember that when you begin to explore ideas in a free-idea exploration, sometimes you may find that the view you did not consider the strongest may, in fact, become the one you believe in and want to write about in a paper.

Directions: Working with your peers, review what you just did and then add more ideas with their help. Because this is practice, just a few new ideas are needed.

Subject _____ persuasive direction you are interested in developing (What would you want to persuade people to consider?) _____
_____

One view of the subject
1. _____
2. _____

An opposite view of the subject
1. _____
2. _____

Remember, the structure for brainstorming a persuasive paper would involve looking at two sides of the same topic. When you are fair about carefully exploring both sides of a persuasive topic using free-idea exploration, you have the potential to write a good and strongly supported paper, because you have a clear understanding of the two sides of the topic.

Peer Discussion

We Are Alike and Different, Too

Using the writing step of brainstorming and using the free-idea exploration for a comparison and/or contrast paper will help you clearly see the similarities and/or differences of any two subjects. Remember that, if you decide to compare things in a paper, you need to understand the similarities and differences between the specific people, events, activities, etc. Certainly, you may choose to write a paper that just compares similarities or just contrasts differences, or both, but when you use free-idea exploration as a method of prewriting brainstorming, you will want to use a brainstorm approach different from the one you used for the persuasive paper.

An example of free-idea exploration for brainstorming a comparison and/or contrast paper is illustrated below. This is a comparison and contrast between friends, and it is for a paper that is comparing likes and differences. Mark and Courtney have been friends since second grade, and they are still good pals. Because they are best friends, it is easy to consider them for a paper topic comparing and contrasting friends. First the similarities will be listed, and then the differences will follow.

Subject: Mark and Courtney - comparing/contrasting best friends

Mark
similarities
in sixth grade
loyal - can be counted on to be a friend
loves baseball, plays catcher
loves to swim, on the swim team
baby in the family - three brothers

differences
male
likes to watch men's sports on television
likes to buy sports equipment
likes to work with machines
likes to hang out with male friends

Courtney
similarities
in sixth grade
loyal - always there to help a friend
loves softball, plays first base
loves to dive, on the diving team
baby in the family - two brothers, one sister

differences
female
likes to watch women's sports on television
likes to buy clothes
likes to baby-sit
likes to hang out with female friends

Once you have listed similarities and differences, you need to evaluate them for potential use as detail to be expanded in a comparison and/or contrast paper. The brainstorming will help you understand what you know about the subject.

Peer Discussion

Name _____

Practice Makes Perfect

Now it is your turn to try this type of brainstorm. First use people you know. Maybe you will want to compare you and your best friend or your sister or brother. This is a good starting point for practice, since you know yourself and you know these people.

Subject: _____

Name_____   Name _____
similarities

_____   _____
_____   _____
_____   _____
_____   _____
_____   _____

differences

_____   _____
_____   _____
_____   _____
_____   _____
_____   _____

Once you fill in these areas, you will know whether or not you have interesting material for a comparison and/or contrast paper.

This prewriting step can be used for events, news situations, activities, rules, or just about anything that can be compared or contrasted. This is the free-idea exploration structure that allows you to brainstorm in a free style before you write.

Peer Discussion

Autobiographies/Biographies

When you write an autobiography, which is a paper about yourself, or a biography, which is a paper about someone else, a successful way to create ideas is to use free-idea exploration. This method allows you to brainstorm without having to worry about paragraph sequence or structure. You can do that later when you frame your paper. But to begin with, just let the ideas take shape. Below is an example of how to form this type of prewriting brainstorm.

Because an autobiography should contain background, life experiences, and goals, you will need to brainstorm all those areas as illustrated in this example. This is an example written by a girl who lives in Michigan.

Background: born in Minneapolis in November the day after a blizzard. Lived in Minneapolis until I was six. Moved to Connecticut for two years. Moved to Indiana for four years and then to Michigan where I live now. Two older sisters, we get along. My name is from an actress that my mother liked before I was born.

Life experiences: like school, won some awards for softball in fourth grade. Traveled to Oklahoma for a vacation and then to Texas to go to an amusement park. Rode the roller coaster 14 times in a row. Involved in community service and help people who are not able to get around. Have a job cutting my neighbor's lawn and baby-sitting my niece. Like not asking for money but earning it myself.

Goals: hope to go to college, hope to become a veterinarian, hope to live in Michigan, and travel the country and Europe. Want to help people and do Special Olympics volunteering when I am old enough. Want to learn sign language. Hope to be a good wife and mother some day and like my life.

These ideas are just in the prewriting phase. They are not meant to be in any particular order or even in complete sentences, since the purpose of this prewriting task is just to get the ideas out and have some information to begin the process of understanding what you know for an autobiography. Free-idea exploration is meant to allow free thought and idea collection before you begin the rough draft preparation. Like the persuasive and comparison and/or contrast paper, it works for the autobiography and biography, too.

Peer Discussion

This Is First and This Is Next . . .

Process writing is an orderly form of writing. The steps for process writing follow one after the other, made easy by using free-idea exploration as a brainstorm method. Process writing is sequential, meaning one step will be the natural transition to the next step, etc. Any task, procedure, or function can easily fit into this writing process function.

For example, if the process is getting ready for school, then the free-idea exploration brainstorm might resemble the following structure.

Subject: Getting ready for school in the morning

Steps:
1. wake up to the alarm, which is my mom telling me to get up
2. getting up and taking a shower and brushing my teeth
3. blow drying my hair
4. putting on makeup
5. choosing what I want to wear to school
6. finding the clothes on my closet floor
7. getting dressed
8. going downstairs to breakfast
9. getting my books and out the door
10. walking to school
11. going to my locker and getting ready for the first class of the day

Each step can easily be developed with more detail once the rough draft is started, but for this part of the writing process, the order of action is in place. Process writing has sequence and order, yet it is easy to use the free-idea exploration to brainstorm a process in preparation for writing. Once you have established order and pattern, adding description and depth will follow in the actual writing.

Peer Discussion

Name _____

Narrative and Reflective Writing

When brainstorming using free-idea exploration for narrative and reflective writing assignments, your brainstorm remains unstructured. For the narrative or reflective assignment, you are simply listing things about your thoughts, feelings, or reactions about a piece of literature, a current event, or a particular historical situation. You will be successful using the structure below when dealing with brainstorming for a narrative or reflective paper.

Subject _____

Details you know about this subject _____
_____
_____
_____
_____

What are your thoughts, feelings, or reactions about this subject? _____
_____
_____
_____
_____

How do those thoughts, feelings, or reactions to the subject relate to real life? _____
_____
_____
_____
_____

From this free-idea exploration, you can take the next step and write a rough draft narrative or reflective paper.

Peer Discussion

Creative Writing

The creative writing free-idea exploration for prewriting brainstorming offers a different structure. When writing a short story, you will want to brainstorm for structure and for detail. It is fun to brainstorm for a short story, since you are the master of the idea and the maker of characters and plot.

An example of how to brainstorm for a creative writing story is illustrated in the example that follows. Then, try your own free-idea exploration by doing the same activity; build a character and make up a story idea all in brainstorm structure.

Creative Writing Assignment: Develop a new character and make up a story for the character.

Main Character: Her name is Trudy, and she is a young girl with brown hair and brown eyes. She is only 8 and, because she was very ill, she is now deaf. She has an older brother and two younger twin sisters. Her mother is a single parent and her father is living away from home, so it is difficult for her mother to take her to sign language classes. They cannot afford for her to go to a residential school. Trudy is a nice girl, but shy.

Plot: The story will be about how Trudy and her family learn sign language and begin to communicate with one another. It will involve her mother and father and her brother and sisters as they learn sign language and about deaf culture. Trudy's father will be back in the story.

Other Characters: Her best friend is Tim, who lives next door. He is nine and hearing. He is a good friend and learns sign language with Trudy. Linda is her cousin and is a year older. She will help Trudy with lip reading and teach her how to ride a bicycle. Her dog, Blondeaux, is a nice dog and helps Trudy when she crosses the street. Blondeaux warns her about cars and other things she may not hear.

Free-idea exploration is open to changes or full sentences or partial ideas. It is prewriting that allows ideas to flow. Whether the actual short story will have all the details that went into this prewriting brainstorm or not, the point is that these ideas are ready for use if needed for the story.

Peer Discussion

Name _____

Directions: Using free-idea exploration, develop a brainstorm for a creative writing short story. Add details as you need them.

Main Character: _____
_____
_____
_____

Plot (what the story will be about): _____
_____
_____
_____
_____

Other characters: _____
_____
_____
_____
_____

There are other sections you may want to add to a brainstorm for a creative short story, such as details about setting (where it will take place) and when and how you are going to end it. Experiment with those other areas in the spaces provided.

Setting: _____
_____
_____

Conclusion: _____
_____
_____

When you are finished filling in the details, you are ready to start a rough draft, since you have a good base on which to build a short story. Brainstorming helps give you direction for that next step.

Prewriting

THE TEACHERS' LOUNGE

Breaking the Ice—Encourage students to reach a comfortable level of interaction in teams or groups by practicing quick group formation to solve simple riddles or answer questions that relate to the work in the classroom. Create groups by simply numbering students and having them form groups (such as even/odd), by requesting that students choose colored strips of paper, or by any other random method.

Once they are in their teams or groups, present questions to the individual teams so that members must work together to answer them. A question might require them to solve riddles from an inexpensive riddle book. Some questions might be generated from the material or short story they just read. Whatever the question, the purpose is to make students solve or find the answer to something, working with students they may not know very well.

The repetitive style of this method will help students to become comfortable with other students in the class and be more secure in offering ideas to people they have just met. When they are assigned to teams for significant and graded work, they will have more confidence to participate.

Free-Idea Exploration: Banners—This chapter deals with the writing process method of brainstorming by free-idea exploration. Assign an activity that can help students realize that this is meant to allow for a free flow of ideas related to a given topic. Acquire either large strips of butcher paper or large pieces of construction paper and assign student teams of two or three per group. Ask students to brainstorm on topics you select that relate to the type of writing you are currently teaching or to some particular unit of study. Ask them to place the topic in the middle of the paper in large letters that can be read from around the room. Then, have them brainstorm in free-idea exploration whatever comes to mind.

Have students of each team present their ideas to the class, and then post the ideas around the room so other students can learn how to brainstorm a topic.

A Handy Task—To encourage more brainstorming and understanding of those brainstorming ideas, ask students to trace their hands on construction paper and then list whatever they want to share with other students in the room about themselves. The hands would be posted around the room. Require at least three background facts, three life experiences, and three goals to help them make an easy step to that type of brainstorming when they do a biography or autobiography free-idea exploration. They will have practice in letting ideas flow, and they will also design something about themselves that will be on display on a wall in the classroom.

CHAPTER THREE
Prewriting
Mapping

TEACHER INFORMATION

Prewriting in the writing process offers other methods of brainstorming. Learning to evaluate whether there is enough information to write a paper about a subject can be accomplished by having students use mapping as a brainstorm technique. A bit more structured than the free-idea exploration, mapping is a method of brainstorming that combines a structure, of sorts, and a level of free-style brainstorming of ideas. Mapping is also known as webbing or clustering, all of which can be considered visual organization. The purpose of this type of prewriting brainstorming is to help students see the relationship between one idea and another and how one idea-filled circle links to another idea circle. Students will begin to understand the sequence of ideas because it is visually easy to view the links and pattern of thought.

Mapping, webbing, and clustering are almost the same process, but *mapping* is the term that will be used throughout this chapter. The student starts with an idea in a circle and develops a branch, or web, or cluster link to other ideas related to the first one and continues this process. When you introduce mapping, webbing, or clustering to students, show them a map, web, or cluster so they see the pattern.

Practicing mapping will provide an opportunity for students to gain confidence in using the procedure. Also, they will have the chance to explore how one idea connects to another and then extends to even more ideas. Mapping provides experience in organization and in thinking skill development.

To begin with, use topics that are familiar to most students. Provided in this chapter will be different examples to use for demonstrating the process. Demonstrating mapping to students will help them make their first attempts using the same process for a subject of interest to them.

Mapping has no particular rules other than the fact that the links have to relate to a core idea or extend from one of the secondary ideas. Staying focused on the subject will help students understand the development of mapping as a successful brainstorming method.

Prewriting: Idea Blossoming

Prewriting is a significant part of the writing process, as it helps students to organize ideas before they actually write their composition or creative assignment. Mapping is a comfortable way for students to see how one idea can lead to another, and how those ideas can blend to become a paper. Also, mapping tends to be less intimidating to students because it is informal in its structure. There is no required format to adhere to other than what common sense and logical thinking dictate.

Mapping in prewriting helps students see that a simple idea can become several good ideas. As they practice the different types of mapping approaches, they will be able to understand the basic format of each type of writing, making it easier for them to transfer that understanding to a written task.

This chapter has many mapping activities, because the more students practice, the more mapping as a prewriting activity will become second nature for projects and papers they complete independently.

Mapping Examples—Reports: This first activity will help students understand mapping and the idea of reports. They will understand that, in order to complete a report, they need to know what they want to write about, and that means they need to do some background work. The example is meant to be basic and illustrate that mapping will work for any given subject.

Mapping Practice—Reports: Choosing a topic matching their own interest will help students experiment with letting an idea blossom into other related ideas. Even if they do not use this particular mapping task, they will have it available for a possible future paper.

Mapping Example—Persuasive: Papers of persuasion are challenging because they require that the student understand both sides of a topic. The mapping example and practice for the persuasive paper allows for the student to view that division.

Mapping Practice—Persuasive: Practice in dividing a topic to understand its power for persuasion is helpful for students. Mapping offers a visual example that is easy for middle school students to understand. When they map their own topic, they will learn to think of supporting detail that will help to develop the purpose of their own paper.

Mapping Example—Compare/Contrast: Compare and/or contrast papers divide into different ideas as do the papers of persuasion. Depending on the purpose of the paper, that division of ideas will embrace similarities or differences, or both. This example will simply help students to understand how to develop their own comparison and/or contrast papers when they are ready to practice writing.

Mapping Practice—Compare/Contrast: Using two of something they know about will help students to develop a good mapping activity in the compare and/or contrast format. This is an effective learning tool for students because, when they are finished, they can see clearly how two items share similar traits and different ones, too.

Mapping Example—Autobiography/Biography: These two types of writing are so similar in their mapping development that they can be covered at the same time. This example illustrates a topic that would be simple for students to follow.

Mapping Practice—Autobiography/Biography: Most students enjoy writing about themselves. They are able to map what they know, and the details should come easily to them. They also learn that there is dimension to an autobiography and biography that includes much more than year of birth and place of birth. This mapping exercise can expand easily.

Mapping Example/Practice—Process: Process writing can become very involved. However, students at the middle school level will probably be comfortable with using daily living activities when choosing to map a process paper topic. Easy in design, the process paper mapping activity is easy to develop.

Mapping Example—Creative Writing: Mapping helps students understand that a creative writing story has many possible angles to it. They may choose to develop a story about a character, a theme, a plot, etc., but the mapping in this prewriting activity can also include descriptive language and elaborate plot detail. Imagination has no limit with this form of prewriting.

Mapping Practice—Creative Writing: Students can have fun with this activity because it is their own imagination that will drive this task. They will have the freedom to develop the mapping for a future creative writing story. Mapping gives them a full view of the many options of their story.

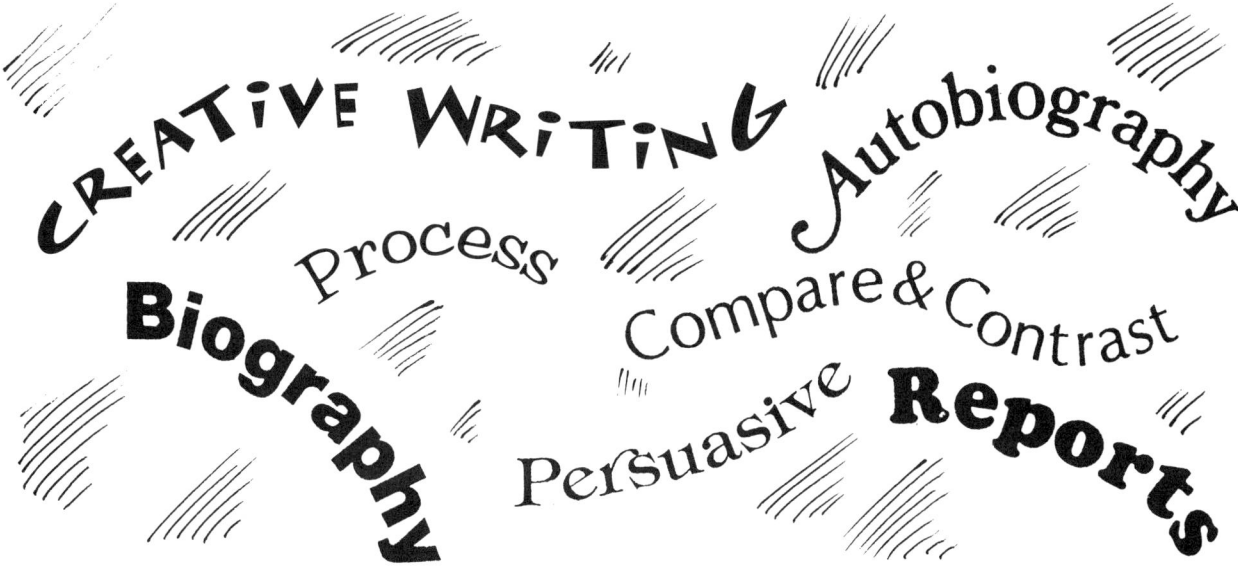

Mapping

Example–Reports

First attempts at mapping will be easier once you understand the basic flow of a map of ideas. Mapping involves beginning with a basic idea and branching out as you consider more ideas related to that core subject.

When mapping a report topic, you might choose a local landmark or institution. For example, if you lived in Rochester, Michigan, you might choose Oakland University in that same city. You would find report information to use in your paper by either surfing the Internet or World Wide Web or by using materials in your school's library. Then you would apply what you learned to the mapping structure. The following mapping example might be the result of such an activity.

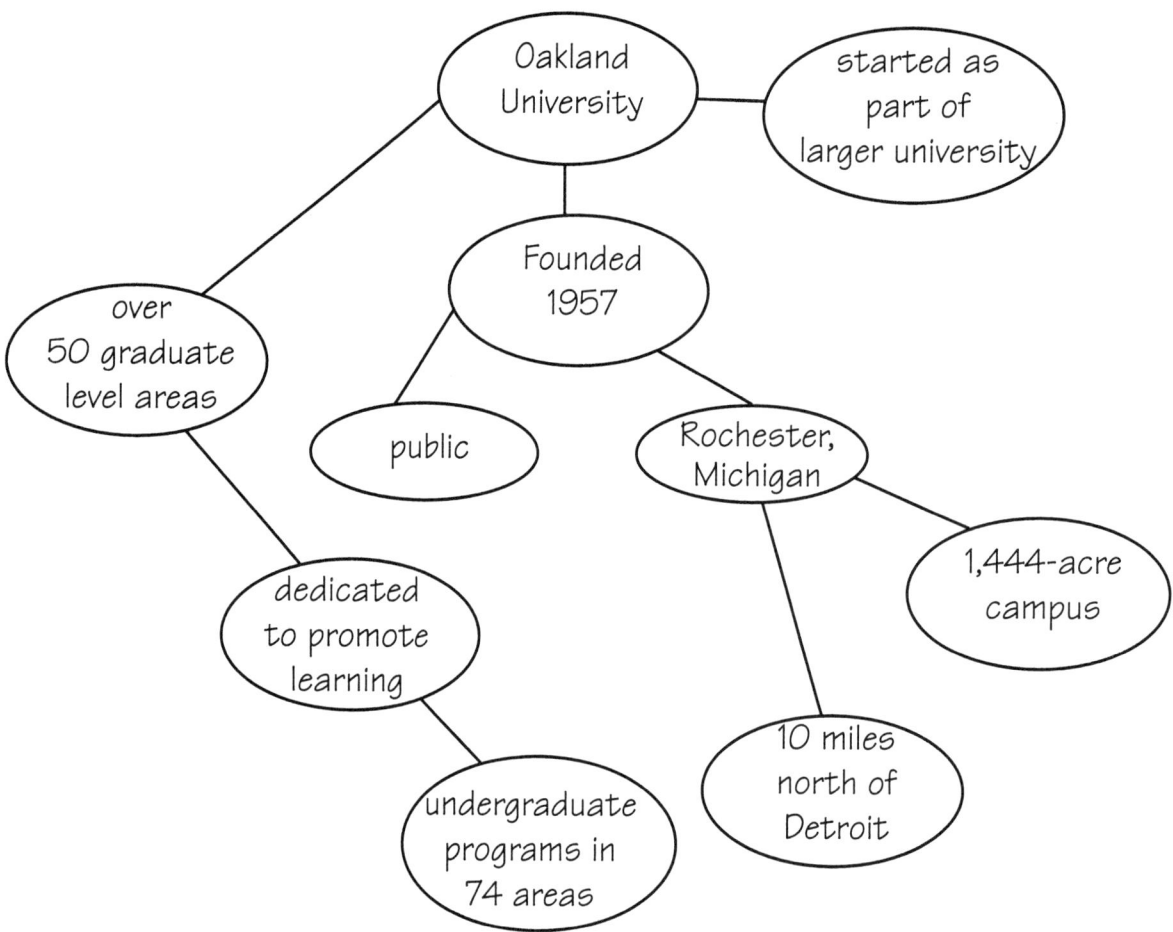

Remember that the next step after mapping is to complete the rough draft writing. With mapping as a prewriting activity, you are now in a position to tackle that next step.

Mapping

Name _____

Practice-Reports

Directions: Practice mapping for your report. First, choose a topic that will be interesting to investigate. Next, find some information about it by either searching the Internet and World Wide Web or by looking for material in the library.

Once you have that material, read through it and learn as much as you can about your topic. At that point, you will have enough knowledge to begin the prewriting brainstorm activity of mapping. The mapping you do here will probably result in a report that you will write and edit for a grade. Consider what you want to cover in your report and the order in which you will place your details.

The topic of your report is _____

Now, develop a mapping of that topic with supporting detail.

This mapping activity will be valuable for your rough draft formation, so keep it handy for the next step in the writing process.

Mapping

Example—Persuasive

The prewriting process of mapping allows you to view both sides of the topic about which you are attempting to persuade your audience. In mapping a topic of persuasion, start with the topic and list details for the pro (in favor of) side and details for the con (against) side. With both sides of the topic clearly listed, you will have a "blueprint" of what areas you need to cover to eventually turn the brainstorm mapping into a rough draft paper.

The process is similar to the mapping for a report except that it will provide two clearly different viewpoints of the topic. Generally, the pro side will have more ideas listed. However, if you find more details on your con side, you may consider switching to that side of the persuasive topic, since it appears that you have a better understanding of that side.

Below is an example of a prewriting mapping brainstorm for a persuasive paper. The topic is whether dogs make better pets than cats. The mapping details both sides of the persuasive idea.

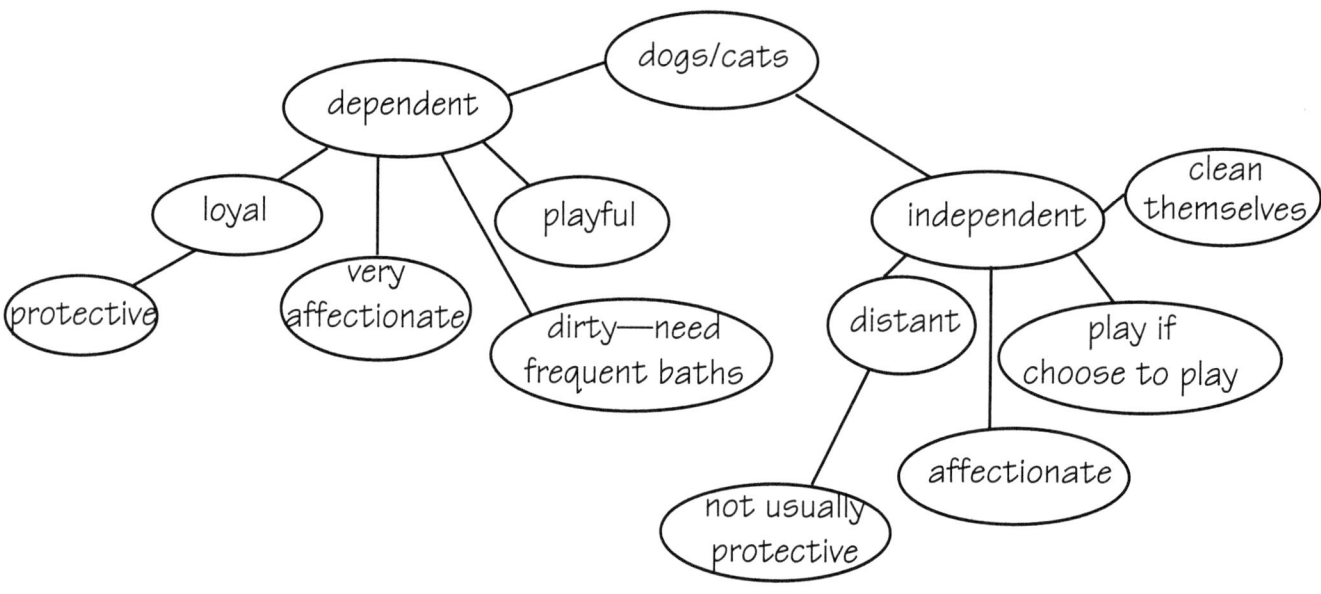

Prewriting using mapping when preparing to write a persuasive paper will help you make a commitment to one side or the other, because you will clearly see both sides before you write.

Mapping

Practice—Persuasive

Directions: Now it is your turn to practice working with prewriting using a mapping brainstorm. First, choose a subject. Remember to select an idea for your paper that has two sides to it. Consider details that will support your topic of persuasion and its opposite view to help understand both sides. Understanding both sides of a persuasive topic means that you have done the work necessary to make a full commitment to your topic.

Topic _____

Mapping:

Once you are finished with mapping your persuasive topic, review the side you want to persuade your audience to believe and make certain that you have covered all the logical details that support your position. This mapping brainstorming will eventually help you to develop a well-thought-out and well-planned paper.

Example—Compare/Contrast

Mapping for a prewriting exercise when preparing to write a comparison and/or contrast paper helps you understand the similarities and differences of the two items you are going to investigate. Mapping helps you to see clearly the details about both sides, no matter what you are comparing and/or contrasting.

Below is an example of how mapping may develop when comparing and/or contrasting two people. The two people are sisters, and the paper would combine both similarities and differences.

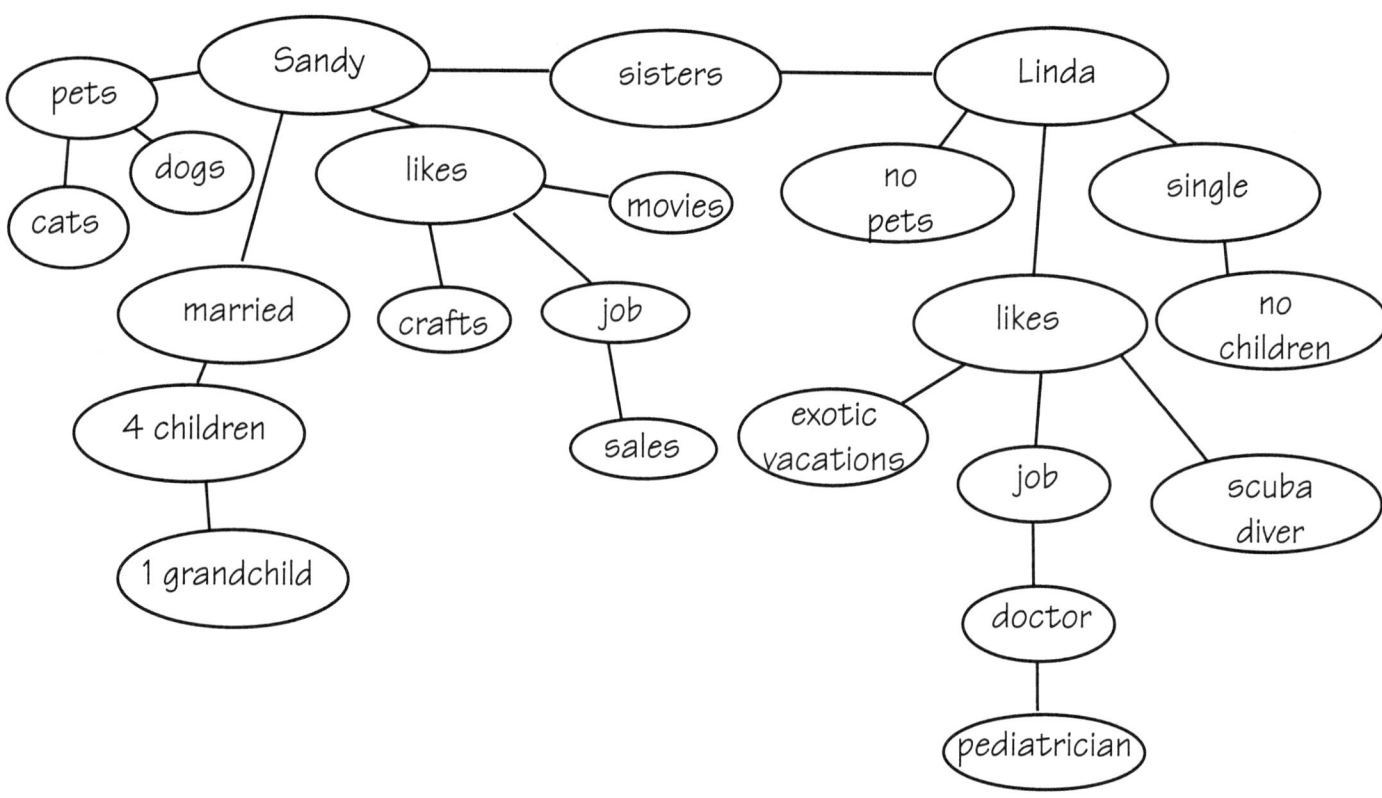

Once the mapping is completed, you should have enough detail to form a solid, well-detailed main body for a paper of comparison and/or contrast.

Mapping

Name _____

Practice–Compare/Contrast

Directions: Practice mapping for a comparison and/or contrast paper. List your topic and then develop a mapping that has two distinct areas to it. This clear division will help you see the similarities and differences of the two things you are comparing and/or contrasting. For topic ideas, consider two people, two countries, two schools, or two objects.

Topic _____

Mapping:

Review the ideas you just mapped for your topic. If you have even more ideas, add them to the mapping activity you just finished. Your next step in the writing process is to use these ideas in the paper you will write.

Mapping

Example–Autobiography/Biography

The autobiography and biography actually share the same structure for the prewriting activity of mapping. The key to using mapping for this type of paper is to remember that there is more to a person's life than just basic facts like date and place of birth. Include successes and achievements, failures, goals, and dreams.

This example is about a man who is an engineer for a large company. He works hard to care for his family, and he volunteers at an art museum once every few months. He is kind to his neighbors and is a good citizen. The topic of the paper is a person who is admired for his commitment to life, so the prewriting mapping could develop like this:

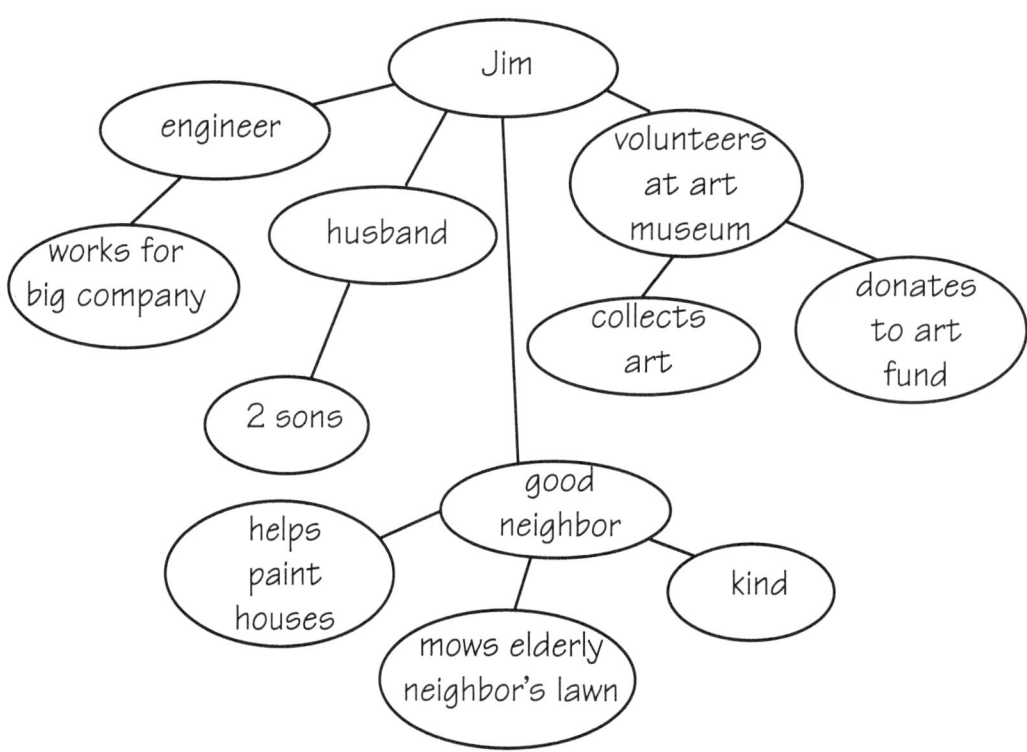

Perhaps all of the information that developed in the mapping activity would not be used, but it is available if it is needed in the development of the rough draft. If your assignment is an autobiography, it could easily follow this format, only it would be about you.

Mapping

Name _____

Practice—Autobiography/Biography

Directions: The mapping structure for prewriting gathering of ideas will develop easily for an autobiography because it is about you. A biography uses the same categories for information gathering, but it is about someone else. Gathering details for a biography will require a bit more research on your part, but once you begin mapping, the same subtopics will be developed as when you map for an autobiography.

For practice, use details about yourself or about someone you know and brainstorm in a mapping style things like birthplace, birth date, interesting childhood events, accomplishments, strengths, goals, and dreams.

Once you are finished gathering details about yourself or about another person, you are ready to write an autobiography or a biography.

Mapping

Name _____

Example/Practice–Process

Process papers easily adapt to the mapping style for prewriting. The key to developing an accurate mapping is to think about all the steps before you write them down and then place them in sequential order.

If you were going to develop a prewriting mapping for the process of doing the dishes after your evening meal, you might develop a map similar to the one listed below:

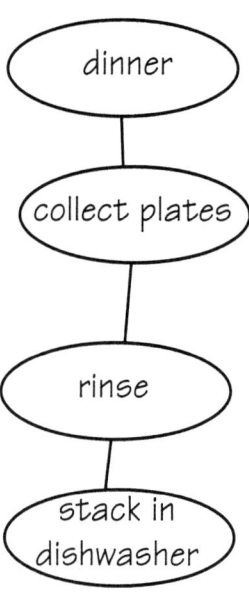

Directions: Practice your own process mapping for something that you do regularly, so you are familiar with the steps. You may choose to list something like getting ready for school, making breakfast, cleaning the kitchen, or making lunch for school. Think carefully and do your mapping above on the right side of this sheet.

Mapping

Example—Creative Writing

Prewriting for a creative writing assignment can result in many different mapping setups, depending on the purpose of your story. You may choose to focus on a character and build the mapping from there. You may develop a story that is a conflict, or a problem, so your mapping would begin with that conflict and branch out from there. You may also develop a creative writing story that is based on fear, happiness, or some other emotion, developing a mapping brainstorm that is mood-based.

The mapping possibilities are as vast as your imagination. Using mapping will help you plan your story so that when you begin to write it, you will have some idea of the basic direction of your story.

The mapping example for this creative writing story is character-focused about a young boy named Timmy who grew up in the suburbs of Atlanta, Georgia. Timmy had a dog named Poochy, and Timmy loved to fish and play tag with his friend, Tom. The boys were best friends.

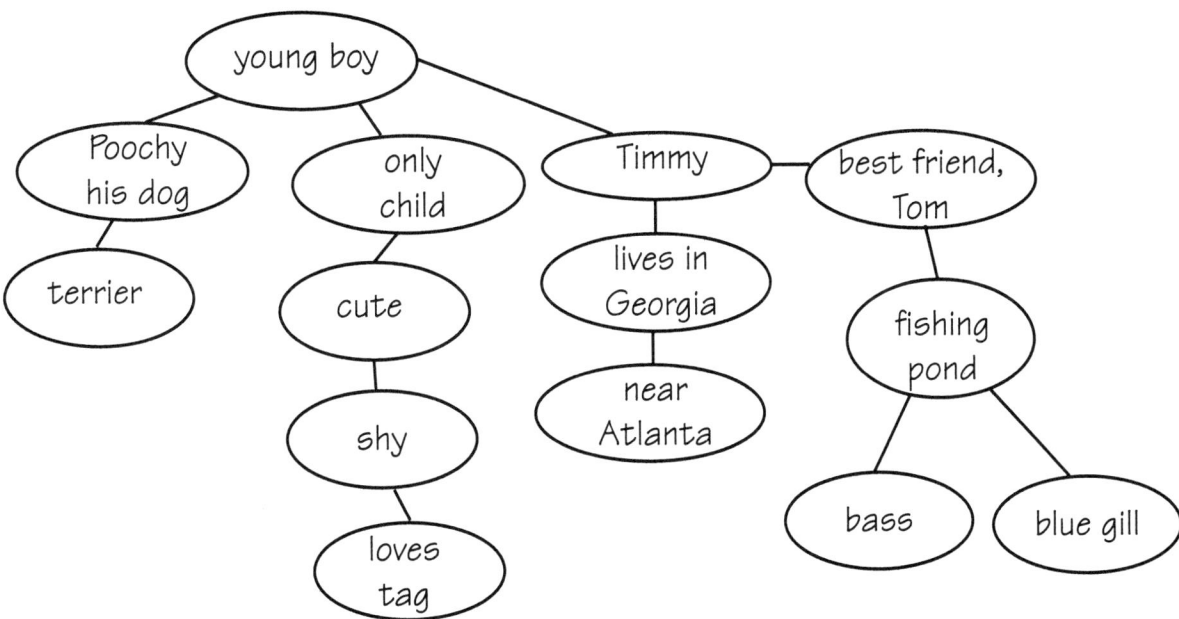

From this point of the prewriting activity, it will be easy to begin to develop an actual story that is character-focused and has a logical sequence to it. Mapping helps to organize the basic ideas.

Mapping

Name _____

Practice—Creative Writing

Directions: Using your imagination, practice mapping a story that is about a character, a problem, a mood, or an event. Include who is in the story, details about those characters, what the story is about, and interesting information. Remember that, although you will develop many ideas in this mapping practice, you want to remain open to new ideas as you actually write the rough draft of your paper.

What is your story about? Briefly detail your basic idea before you begin to map it.

_____
_____

Begin mapping below:

Once you have finished mapping your creative writing short story, review it to see if you want to add more in a particular section. When you finish that, you will be ready to write the actual story.

Prewriting
THE TEACHERS' LOUNGE

Mapping for prewriting organization is a positive way for students to see the path of an idea. It helps them understand where their idea begins and how it can evolve into additional ideas and become a "blueprint" for a rough draft paper. Students enjoy mapping because it is free of boundaries and confined structure, and ideas flow from one another.

Hey, Here's an Idea!—Each week hang a large sheet of paper cut into the shape of a huge light bulb somewhere in the room. Place a core topic in the center of the light bulb and, as students finish their work, invite them to consider mapping ideas that could extend from the core idea. Students write on the light bulb sheet and build on the idea during the week.

At the beginning of each class, review what students have written to encourage them to think about mapping subjects. Because the input is student-generated, everyone will have the opportunity to see how mapping develops.

At the end of each week, review and roll up the mapping exercise and store it for use in a few weeks. Once you have enough light bulbs, divide your class into teams of two or three students and have them randomly choose one of the light bulb tubes. As a team writing task, they can use the prewriting mapping developed by the class to create a rough draft composition on whatever topic they selected. They will know the topic, since it was the light bulb activity of the week, and they probably participated in the development of those ideas. Team writing means they can gain practice in using a mapping exercise to create a paper, and they have other students who can help in its development.

The New Student—Trace a person's shape, or use a shape like a full-size gingerbread man, on butcher paper or on several pieces of construction paper. Tape that shape to the back of the classroom door or a wall that is protected from student traffic.

As the week progresses, invite students to fill in the form with either information about an author they may be studying or different details about themselves. You will have the mapping for a biography or an autobiography and, if they do a collective effort, it will be interesting to students to see the similarities and differences among students in the class.

Suggest that students use different colored pencils for areas relating to facts, traits, accomplishments, goals, and dreams. You may choose to assign the mapping of dreams and goals to the head area and the basic facts to the torso area. Traits might be mapped in the arms and legs and goals in the hands. Of course, the mapping can be anywhere on the cutout. It is a matter of personal taste.

On the feet of the cutout, encourage students to add sophisticated vocabulary for description of a person. Words that relate to personality, characteristics, traits, and goals could be found in an assignment working with a thesaurus. This focused vocabulary searching would provide exposure to the thesaurus.

Cartoon Mapping Practice—Save some Sunday comics from the local newspaper for a few weeks and then bring them to class. Place students into teams of no more than three. They will practice using the comic section for mapping practice. First, they need to find a cartoon series of at least four frames and read it. They can discuss the story of the cartoon and the purpose of it before they map the cartoon.

Next, they can use a piece of unlined paper and map the cartoon. They need to find the core idea of the cartoon and map in the characters involved, how they seem to know each other, what they look like, what they are doing, what they are sharing as an activity or a problem, and the outcome of that interaction.

They may do this with several cartoons. This activity provides another visual approach to the mapping process. Also, it provides a positive experience for students learning to work together as a team.

CHAPTER FOUR
Prewriting
Listing and Outlining

TEACHER INFORMATION

Prewriting offers other ways to organize ideas before approaching the rough draft. Students will benefit from learning techniques involved in listing and outlining.

Listing is simply putting down ideas that would logically follow one another. Unlike mapping, listing is free of circles and linking lines. Listing starts with one topic idea and then, as the student brainstorms, the list of corresponding and related ideas will follow. A list can be short or long, depending on the idea and the level of knowledge of the subject.

If the list is too short, it may mean that the student needs to do more research to find out more about the subject. Listing will help students understand whether they need to do more work to prepare to compose a paper or composition before they begin that task.

Outlining is a formal prewriting activity and is worth review. However, because outlining has a formal structure and is more precise, it tends to be more challenging for some students at the middle school level. With an understanding of how to do mapping and listing, outlining may not be a choice students at that level may seek. Yet, an introduction or review of outlining is worthwhile.

Outlining has steps and numbering and requires a consistent pattern. When those steps are precisely followed, a pattern of subject ideas develops, helping the student to prepare for rough draft writing. As challenging as it may be, outlining does help students understand the initial core idea and the various steps for composition development.

Whether a student chooses mapping from the last chapter or listing and outlining as explained in this chapter, the results will be the same. The student will be able to use one of these prewriting approaches to prepare for the next step in the writing process of rough draft construction.

Lists and Outlines, Too

The activities in this chapter will help students to develop better papers and compositions. This chapter extends the prewriting phase of the writing process by exploring the use of listing and outlining as activities for brainstorming. Once students are comfortable with turning an idea into a "blueprint" for writing, they can move to the next phase of the writing process and actually write the paper.

Before they can make the transition from prewriting to drafting, they need practice in taking an idea and turning it into a possible writing topic. Listing and outlining will help them to make that transition.

Listing for the Report: This activity provides beginning exposure to the listing process when dealing with a report topic. It helps students see how a simple idea can be developed by listing. This activity provides a model for their own use when dealing with listing as a prewriting process.

Listing for the Persuasive Paper: This activity helps students to understand how listing will allow them to see both sides of a persuasive topic. Once they see two sides to their persuasive idea, students should be able to understand the level of persuasion they need to develop in a paper.

Listing for Comparison and/or Contrast: Like the persuasion topic, this activity provides two sides to the chosen topic. Listing both sides for comparison and/or contrast topics helps students to develop well-planned and organized papers that contain details for comparison or for contrast or for both styles.

Listing for Autobiography and Biography: This activity helps students understand the depth of investigation that is needed for an autobiographical or biographical paper. Listing for this type of writing helps them to find good details for use in their paper.

Listing for the Narrative, Reflective, and Process Papers: The narrative listing practice helps students to better understand the personal level of the narrative. The reflective section helps students move to a more inferential level of thinking about the topic. The process listing practice helps students logically consider particular steps in a process.

Listing for the Creative Writing Paper: Creative writing papers involve more than just writing what a student may feel at that moment. This activity helps students to understand the depth of a creative writing short story. It gives them practice in brainstorming for a short story. Like any other style of paper, using the prewriting activity of listing helps them to expand their ideas to a level that will encourage a better creative writing task.

Outlining: Although outlining tends to be formal and is not necessarily a favorite with most students, this section provides some exposure to the development of an outline. Topic and sentence style outlines are illustrated in this activity. Some students may find this style of prewriting brainstorming the most efficient and useful of all the prewriting activities. Outlining is precise and accurate, and it does help with the actual planning of a paper. Although many students may favor mapping and listing, exposure to outlining provides a third method for them to choose when prewriting for a composition.

Listing

Report

Listing follows the identification of your topic. Once you establish a topic for your paper, assess what you know about your subject. Listing will establish what you know and what you need to learn to develop a complete and organized paper.

First, decide what your topic will be for the paper. Depending on the type of paper you are writing, listing may follow a few different paths. For example, a paper that is a report will have a simple listing of detail like the one that follows. The actual process of listing will be spontaneous brainstorming of what you know about the subject. Once your listing is completed, review what you just wrote to help you begin to frame your paper and eventually write the rough draft. This level of the writing process is easy because you simply list details.

A report, which is a paper that provides information, may have a listing like the following:

Report Topic: Dinosaurs

on the planet over 200 million years ago . . . two types—meat eaters and plant eaters . . . dinosaurs came in all sizes from small to huge . . . lived on earth for millions of years . . . they are extinct . . . many theories of why they died . . . but it was final and deadly to dinosaurs

Next, decide if there is enough information to write a report for your class assignment. If, after you review what you wrote, you learn that you needed more information, you have to go to the library and do some research on dinosaurs or use the Internet and World Wide Web and surf for some extra details. Listing provides you with an understanding of what you already knew about a topic.

Whatever the topic, listing helps you clearly see topic details you may choose to use in a report for class.

Listing

Name _____

Directions: Now it is your turn to try listing for a report. You know a lot about many things and you may not even realize it. Listing helps you to understand just what you know. This prewriting activity in the writing process helps you to slow your mind and let ideas about a particular subject surface so that you can write them down to be used in a report.

As practice to prove what you know, the following subjects are pretty basic, and you will be surprised at what you do know once you begin to list details about them. Relax and let your mind generate the details you know about each subject or category and then list them below each topic. This activity may be used for writing a future report, or it may spark your interest to learn more about one of these topics.

Topic: Automobiles

_____
_____
_____
_____
_____

Topic: A Sport

_____
_____
_____
_____
_____

Topic: A Music Group

_____
_____
_____
_____
_____

Topic: A Movie Star

_____
_____
_____
_____
_____

This practice should help you realize that you know a lot about many things. Report prewriting listing helps you understand what you do know and what you still need to learn before you begin the rough draft of your paper.

Persuasive Paper

Persuasive papers attempt to convince the reader to agree with a particular belief, theory, or attitude about a given topic. Unlike a report, the persuasive paper has a more direct goal of proving something and, eventually, persuading the reader to believe what is being proven.

The prewriting activity of listing helps you understand what it is you want to persuade and what you may still need to investigate to develop a strong paper. Listing helps you clearly see what you know and what you may still need to learn before you begin to write your paper.

The persuasive listing may use two approaches. It may simply list the actual points of persuasion, or it may list both sides of the same topic. If it is simply a listing of actual points that will be used to persuade, then probably you are comfortable with that topic and that argument. However, if you need to look at both sides before you decide which direction of persuasion you want to use, then it will be best for you to list details about both positions.

A persuasive paper convinces the reader to believe something about a given topic. The following example illustrates how a topic of persuasion may be developed in the prewriting structure of listing for choosing one side of a topic.

Persuasive Topic: Chewing gum should be banned in school.

students stick it under desks . . . it ends up on the floor and on shoes . . . the wrappers litter the building . . . students blow bubbles in class and make noise chewing gum . . . students chomp on the gum when giving a speech

Next is the same topic with two sides listed.

Persuasive Topic

A: Chewing gum should be banned in school.
   students stick it under desks
   it ends up on the floor and on shoes
   the wrappers litter the building
   students blow bubbles in class and make
     noise chewing gum
   students chew gum when giving a speech

B: Chewing gum should be allowed in school.
   students are responsible
   students can clean the building
   the wastebasket is handy
   it can be chewed quietly
   it can be removed for a speech

Listing

Name _____

Directions: Now it is your turn to practice using listing for a persuasive topic. First, choose a topic of persuasion for this prewriting activity. Remember that you want a stronger topic than a report topic. You are not just going to report or write about a subject; you are going to persuade the reader to believe your theory or idea.

You may choose a current event that has a "right or wrong" feeling to it, such as a political decision, a change of a law, or an unfair situation in a country, a state, or your city. You may choose a rule that is in place in your school or in your home. You may choose a decision made for a sports team or a group of some sort. It may be a topic of debate, such as whether a particular habit should be broken or whether people should believe one way or another regarding life choices. The decision is up to you, but you need to choose a topic and then do the following to practice listing.

This activity may lead to a well-developed paper that you may choose to submit to your teacher in a class, so be serious and think carefully about what you think will help support your topic.

First, try listing only one side of a topic.

Topic: _____

_____

_____

_____

_____

Next, try another topic but experiment with both sides to determine which side you feel would develop into a stronger paper of persuasion.

Topic: _____

_____

_____

_____

_____

Topic: _____

_____

_____

_____

_____

Listing

Compare/Contrast

The comparison and/or contrast paper is easy to list for prewriting. Once you decide on your subject, you simply list either similarities or differences or both between two items, people, events, places, etc.

Comparison and/or contrast is like a report and a persuasive paper combined. You are working with two subjects but combining them into one. You may just report about the two different subjects or you may choose to contrast them and persuade your reader to believe that one side is better than the other. That choice is up to you.

The following is an example of a comparison and/or contrast listing. The topic is cats and dogs.

Topic: Cats and Dogs

Cats	Dogs
respond when they want to	generally will come when called
love to play with string	love to play with sticks and balls
can be left in the house all day	need to go outside during the day
fairly quiet	may bark a lot
affectionate but on their terms	generally affectionate all the time
can be mean	can be mean
can be great pets	can be great pets

This prewriting listing allows you to consider your next step before you begin to write a rough draft for your paper. With the listing in place, you can decide if you want to develop a comparison paper, a comparison/contrast paper, or just a contrast paper regarding cats and dogs. The option is yours, as you now have a clear understanding of your topic's details.

Listing

Name _____

Directions: Using the comparison and/or contrast approach, practice prewriting listing on two subjects of your choosing. Your topics may include two friends, matching your brother or sister to yourself, your parents, two schools, two states, two religions, or two historical events. The combinations are as vast as your imagination.

In preparation, take a few minutes and list several topics that are natural for comparing or contrasting or both.

_____ and _____   _____ and _____

_____ and _____   _____ and _____

Choose one set and then fill in the following to gain practice in using listing as a prewriting activity for comparison and/or contrast.

Topic _____   Topic _____

_____   _____
_____   _____
_____   _____
_____   _____
_____   _____
_____   _____

After you complete the listing, examine the ideas you used. Examining the details helps you decide if you are going to write a paper that compares two items, contrasts them, or does both. The decision should be based on what types of details you decided to use from your listing.

Listing

Name _____

Autobiography and Biography

Prewriting listing for an autobiography or biography is similar to listing for a report. Simply choose to write about yourself or someone else. List details under that topic to help you determine what you know about the topic. When you do this, you can investigate your topic and determine if you have enough information to develop a full paper.

If you do not have enough detail about yourself for your autobiography, seek information from family and friends. If you do not have enough information about a particular person for a biography, interview if the person is alive or research in the library or Internet if he/she is famous and died long ago.

Be accurate with your details and remember to include details that are more than just facts.

Autobiographies and biographies are papers about people. They deal with actual facts and ideas about people.

Directions: Practice listing for an autobiography or biography below. First, list for an autobiography (about yourself). Next, list for a biography (about another person).

Topic _____
    _____
_____
_____
_____
_____
_____

Topic _____
    _____
_____
_____
_____
_____
_____

Listing

Narrative, Reflective, and Process Papers

Narrative, reflective, and process papers all benefit from listing in the prewriting phase of the writing process. The narrative may relate a personal experience, the reflective may detail ideas, beliefs, or reactions to life experiences, and the process paper may detail steps to completing a task or activity. All three styles of writing have a beginning, a middle, and an end.

Listing for all three styles of writing may result in the following prewriting activities. To demonstrate how the listing activities may develop, all three examples of the individual styles will deal with the topic of moving to a new neighborhood.

The narrative deals with the actual event, the experience of moving, so its listing activity might look like the following:

Narrative
Topic: moving to a new neighborhood

In fifth grade living in Arizona
Dad came home and told us about his job transfer
putting the house up for sale and having people look at our house
traveling to Maine to buy a new house and seeing the new city
moving day and the packing of the truck

There is enough detail provided in that listing to make the switch to writing a rough draft.

The reflective paper deals with reactions to things, so the listing for that type of paper is similar to the narrative. However, rather than relating the memory of the moving experience, the reflective paper might deal with the emotional and reactive feelings about moving. This listing could look like the following:

Reflective
Topic: moving to a new neighborhood

feeling uneasy about leaving a lifelong neighborhood
loss of home and strangeness of new city
feelings about having the house sold
dealing with loss of childhood friends
making new friends and dealing with shyness

Listing

Once again, with the listing for the reflective paper, the next step in developing the rough draft makes more sense. That listing will help develop the paper.

Finally, the process listing details an aspect of the move itself. It may deal with the steps involved to sell a house and actually move to a new location, or it may deal with some other process of the move.

Process
Topic: moving to a new neighborhood

notify the real estate company to arrange the sale . . . contact the movers to arrange a moving date . . . scout out the new city and arrange to find a home . . . register at the new school . . . return to pack and prepare to move to the new city

Listing for the narrative, the reflective, and the process papers helps you to organize your ideas in a logical way. You are still brainstorming, but you are just putting those brainstorm ideas down as they develop. You do not have to worry about where they belong or how they match a certain idea or link. From that brainstorming listing activity, you should be able to develop a good rough draft paper.

Directions: Now it is your turn to try your skill at listing. For each one of the types of writing styles, brainstorm and list ideas. For this first attempt, it might be best to work with a partner or two so that you can share ideas as you try your hand at brainstorming for listing.

The first style to brainstorm and list is the narrative. Remember, this is the type of paper that relates a personal experience. You and your team members are in a wonderful time of life filled with similar experiences. Decide what to brainstorm by sharing ideas to find a common experience. Consider things like your impression of attending middle school, getting used to middle school and its rules and the volume of homework, joining a club, or going out for a team sport. Once you decide what topic to use, then brainstorm and fill in the narrative listing activity on the next page. Remember, listing helps you to understand what you know about a topic in preparation for writing.

Listing

Name _____

Narrative—Topic: _____

Listing detail: _____

_____

_____

_____

_____

The next style is the reflective paper. The reflective paper deals with reactions to things, so you may choose to brainstorm with your team members your reactions to being a student in middle school, your feelings about the increase in homework and other obligations, or your feelings about clubs or sports. Whatever the topic, discuss it with your team and then list ideas that might be useful in a reflective paper.

Reflective—Topic: _____

Listing detail: _____

_____

_____

_____

_____

Your third practice activity is the process paper listing. Dealing with actual details of a process, your team may want to consider something like getting your school materials organized in your backpack, planning how to approach homework tasks, or listing the steps to accomplish a task for a club or a sport. Brainstorm for a process topic and then fill in the following prewriting listing.

Process—Topic: _____

Listing detail: _____

_____

_____

_____

_____

Listing in the prewriting stage of the writing process offers you the opportunity to understand your depth of knowledge for a paper. It offers you the chance to find out if you know enough about your topic to develop a paper on that subject. Taking your time to brainstorm and list details for narrative, reflective, and process papers will help you prepare for the rough draft construction of your paper.

Listing

Name _____

Creative Writing

Directions: Develop a prewriting listing of ideas for writing a creative short story. Whether you do this alone or with a partner, consider each area carefully and add information and ideas as you think of them.

If you see descriptions, like your character has big blue eyes and blonde hair, then list those details in the appropriate category as you think of them. This will help you imagine your character before you actually write your story. This prewriting planning should help you stay organized when you begin to write your story.

Short story topic—what is your story idea? _____

Setting—where will it take place (give some details)? _____
_____
_____

Plot—what is the story about? _____
_____
_____
_____

Characters—what are some details about them? _____
_____
_____
_____

Conflict—what problems are in the story? _____
_____
_____

Solution to the problems—how are they solved? _____
_____
_____

This prewriting activity will provide a good framework for a well-built story. Think carefully about each area and jot down ideas as they occur to you. Working with this part of the writing process will provide an easy method for you to develop a full creative writing assignment.

© Instructional Fair • TS Denison

Listing

Listing helps to organize your creative story ideas. Creative writing stories are a lot of fun to write, but they also require the need to control an idea if it is to become a developed story. When you are given the assignment of writing a short story, listing will help you see your story before you begin to write it. Listing will help you to control the direction of your story idea, your plot, the development of your characters, the building of believable problems, and the solving of those problems. Listing will help you write a good short story.

When you begin to brainstorm and list for a creative writing assignment, let your imagination go as you list the ideas that pop into your mind. Also list areas to brainstorm like where it would take place, what it would be about, who would be in your story, what they would look like, and how they would behave. Include problems they would face and how they would solve those problems. The brainstorm will help you think through your story before you actually start to write it, and the result will be a story that was obviously well planned. That makes for a better story.

For example, if the story is about a boy named Mark, the brainstorm listing might develop as follows:

Setting: a small city in northern Michigan, nice cabin, woods all around, lakes to fish, rivers to canoe, the year does not matter.

Plot: the story is about Mark and his desire to learn how to cross-country ski. The story would focus on his desire to buy skis but no money to use and no idea how to make money to buy them.

Characters: Mark, 11, dark hair, dark brown eyes. He has a sister named Angeline and a brother named Christopher. He is a responsible boy and he would never take anything that did not belong to him. Mark likes to solve problems. Angeline builds birdhouses to sell, and Christopher is just a toddler.

Problem/conflict: Mark wants to buy a pair of cross-country skis, but he has no money.

Solution of the problem: Mark will baby-sit for his brother, Christopher, and receive a share of the profit from selling the birdhouses. Everyone is happy.

This brainstorm is basic, but it would help to develop a rough draft for a creative writing story. More description and details would be added as the story developed in full rough-draft style.

Outlining

Outlining is another technique that you can use in the prewriting stage of the writing process. Outlining is more exact than the mapping or listing techniques that you just learned and practiced using. Outlining has a set pattern and procedure. Although the outlining illustrated on this page is very basic, it can become quite elaborate and extensive. Outlining will help you organize your thoughts about a given topic and put them in a logical order.

Outlining can be used for most styles of compositions and papers, but it tends to be most useful when dealing with reports, persuasive, narrative, reflective, and process papers. These tend to become more specific and will benefit from outlining.

An outline may develop in several ways, but the common styles are the topic outline and the sentence outline. The topic outline uses core ideas that will eventually be developed into full paragraphs in the rough draft. Free of details, the topic outline covers only topics that will be used in the paper. This type of outline really deals with main body ideas, as the introductory paragraph and the concluding paragraph are usually not included in the outline.

An example of a topic outline for a report about England might develop as follows:

Topic: England
I. History
   A. Royalty
   B. Explorers
   C. Notable Englishmen

II. Art
   A. Fine Art
   B. Literature
   C. Music

III. Politics
   A. Royalty
   B. Democracy

Listing

The topic outline will help you develop a rough draft paper, once you establish which topic areas you will write about in your report. It helps you understand your paper's direction.

The sentence outline is different from the topic outline because it offers more details. The sentence outline encourages the development of a sentence style, although complete sentences are not necessarily used. Like the topic outline, the sentence outline usually does not include the introductory paragraph or the concluding paragraph; it displays only the main body of the paper.

An example of a sentence outline is found below. The topic of England also will be used for the sentence outline to demonstrate different approaches to the same idea. The sentence outline is more specific. The phrases in each section conform to a certain pattern.

Topic: England

I. The history behind the development of England
    A. the influence of royalty that shaped the country
    B. the success of explorers that changed the history of England
    C. the impact of notable Englishmen on England's development

II. The acceptance of art in English culture
    A. the embracing of fine art in English culture
    B. the cultivation of literature in England
    C. the influence of music on English society

III. The impact of politics on the shaping of England
    A. the development of England from royalty rule
    B. the emergence of democracy in England

Whether you choose to use the topic outline or the sentence outline, using an outline for prewriting planning will help you to carefully assess the areas that need to be developed in the paper.

Like mapping or listing, the outline will encourage you to understand what you want to write about in each paragraph. With the outline, you will have a sense of what section of the main body to develop first, what section to develop second, etc. Unlike mapping or listing, the outline does present a precise sense of order for the main body. However, unlike the mapping and listing prewriting activities, outlining tends to require more careful planning because of its exacting structure.

Listing

Name _____

Whatever the choice, whether it is mapping, listing, or outlining, this prewriting brainstorming will almost guarantee the development of a good and organized paper. Prewriting helps to develop good compositions.

Outlining will be easier once you practice it a few times. Outlining tends to work best with a lengthy report, a research paper, or a science or social studies project. The more you practice, the better you will be with organizing ideas in an outline format.

Directions: Choose a subject that interests you or that you know a lot about and develop a topic outline for it. Remember that you want to stay in topic style, so avoid writing sentences or long phrases in the outline.

Topic _____

I. _____
   A. _____
   B. _____
   C. _____

II. _____
   A. _____
   B. _____
   C. _____

III. _____
   A. _____
   B. _____
   C. _____

Certainly you may add more details when outlining for your own paper, but for practice this length will provide experience in writing a topic outline. If you need to, refer to the example about England for help.

Listing

Name _____

Next, do the same with a sentence outline, using the same topic.

I. _____
   A. _____
   B. _____
   C. _____

II. _____
   A. _____
   B. _____
   C. _____

III. _____
   A. _____
   B. _____
   C. _____

There are more advanced methods for developing an outline for the prewriting stage of the writing process. There are outlines that have structures like the following one.

Subject _____

I. _____
   A. _____
      1. _____
      2. _____
   B. _____
      1. _____
      2. _____
   C. _____
      1. _____
      2. _____

They can also become even more involved than this. But, no matter how simple or how complex, the outline is a good way to organize ideas before you write the first draft of your paper.

Prewriting

THE TEACHERS' LOUNGE

Practice in listing and outlining will make students stronger when they perform prewriting tasks using the writing process. There are opportunities for your students to practice listing and thinking skills, too.

Movies to List or Outline: When students are watching a movie, have them practice listing as they watch. Since you will be choosing the movies to be viewed in class, you can preview them and jot down headers for the different parts or events in the films. Doing a little previewing preparation for the listing task, you can explain the headers to students so that they are prepared to hear those details as each movie progresses. Also, depending on your group, you may choose to tell them to jot down particular details as a movie develops from one event to the next.

As the school year continues, listing from movies you show in class may become a common activity, because it provides practice in prewriting, note-taking and listening skills, and focused viewing.

Stories to List or Outline: As in the previous activity, listening to stories you read in class will give students a chance to practice either listing or outlining. If you want to encourage growth in both skills, then you may choose to have students alternate between listing and outlining.

When you assign a story for the class to read and analyze, require that they either list or outline, too. This provides good practice with material they will study and have easy access to if they missed listing a section of the story.

Topics List: Build a topics section on the bulletin board and make certain that students know where it is and what it is for. Its purpose would be to expand their awareness of various topics so that they break the routine of writing about the same topics.

Once you announce what the topics board is for, provide a stack of different colored strips of paper. Students can write possible topics on them and turn them in to you for viewing and approval. Once you have approved a topic, place it on the topics board and have students write about it if there is time to do so.

CHAPTER FIVE
Drafting
Framing and First Drafts

TEACHER INFORMATION

Students will be prepared to move to writing their first drafts once they have become comfortable with the process of idea searching and prewriting through mapping, listing, or outlining. The next step in the writing process involves framing their paper and drafting their first copy.

Framing means imagining and planning how they will develop their paper. What they will put in the first paragraph, how many paragraphs their main body will have, and how they will conclude it are all parts of framing.

Framing can be discussed in a team with their peers and actually charted on paper. Framing can be included in your assignment explanation, if you wish to dictate the number of paragraphs and how they should be developed. Also, framing can be imagined by students as they make the transition from the prewriting step to the rough draft step.

Whatever method they may choose, framing is as necessary for the development of a composition as an architectural drawing is for the construction of a house, or an x-ray is before an invasive surgery. Framing allows the student an opportunity to visualize the paper before writing has begun. That visualization does not mean that there can be no deviation from a framed number of paragraphs. On the contrary, the paragraphs may vary and the paper may change once the actual writing takes place. However, framing gives the student a sense of the writing task's dimension and depth. That understanding helps the student to pace the ideas and fit them into the appropriate place in the composition.

Framing also helps students to make a fair assessment about what they know and whether they need still more details for a full composition or paper. If they see that they need a certain number of paragraphs to complete the task, but they do not know enough about their subject, they will know to seek out more information before they write.

The actual drafting of the composition should be relatively painless if your students have followed the writing process steps to this point. First, they have discussed the topic and its ideas in a comfortable peer group interaction. Next, they have completed a prewriting exercise by mapping or listing or outlining. The framing of their composition is the step that happens just before they begin the actual drafting of their paper. They should be prepared to make this step if they have been diligent with the other steps in the writing process. The writing process helps them to approach with confidence the next step of rough draft construction.

Drafting: Weaving Ideas
This chapter weaves all the prewriting work together to develop a rough draft. If students have been careful in their planning in the other sections of the writing process, they are prepared to take this step.

The activities in this section differ from the previous ones, because it is actually time for students to write. In this chapter they learn to understand the basic structure and sequence of their paper rather than just participate in activities. The emphasis is on developing the rough draft. This is an intellectually challenging part of the writing process, but if students have done the preliminary work from the other chapters, they are ready to write their paper.

Framing Focus: This activity helps students to begin to see the structure of their paper. The prewriting of mapping, listing, and outlining should help them to make the next step to more involved idea planning and organizing.

The more practice students have in framing, no matter what the paper topic or style, the better they will become in organizing, sequencing, and paper planning. Also, they can practice peer discussion with these activities. They will gain skill at working as a team and learning how others create and develop ideas.

Rough Draft Construction: This activity and the explanation provide students with an opportunity to master the organizational skills for writing. They should be ready to write the rough draft, so this section will help them understand some of the basic rules for construction.

Rough draft construction must allow some freedom for mistakes. Once students learn that it is okay to scribble out ideas and remove whole paragraphs and rewrite them, they will gain confidence with rough draft construction. The important thing for them to remember here is that they need to maintain focus and organization if they want their paper to have logical sequence.

Rough Draft First Steps: This section helps students get started writing the paper.

Rough Draft—the Whole Package: The drafting step of the writing process is explained in this section. There is a beginning, a middle, and an end to any paper, and this part of the chapter helps students grasp that concept.

To the Student

The last few chapters have helped you prepare for this step of actually writing your rough draft. At this point in the writing process, you have experienced work in a team situation. You have discussed ideas until you were able to develop them into possible writing topics. You have brainstormed through mapping, listing, and outlining, and now you are ready to frame your paper and begin to write it.

The next step in the writing process will help you to develop a graphic idea of how you think your paper should be written. When you frame, you will consider your introductory paragraph, how many main body paragraphs you will need to adequately explain, prove, or develop your topic, and how you will end your paper. Framing will be your writing "blueprint."

After you frame, you will actually write your paper. This is the step in the writing process where all the hard work you have done in preparation will become an actual composition. With all the preparation work you have completed to this point, you should be able to develop a well-written paper.

Some terms that will help you through this step of the writing process include the following:

Framing is the graphic representation of how you feel your paper should develop. It involves shaping your paper by making an educated guess about how many paragraphs will be necessary to write about your topic. Framing can be developed by you and your ideas, or your teacher may set up rules or guidelines for you to follow. Whatever the case, framing helps you see your paper before it is written.

Drafting is putting together a composition or paper. It is pulling your ideas together into a completed form.

The rough draft is the composition or paper in its first form. Like the construction site of a new house, it will be messy and look like it is not finished. That messiness and under-construction look simply show that you are thinking about your topic and improving your ideas as you write. The rough draft is your first attempt at forming your ideas into a completed paper. It is rough and brimming with your fresh ideas.

The final draft is the finished product. Final draft polishing occurs later in the writing process. The goal of the rough draft is to develop a paper that will soon become a final polished and organized paper.

Framing

Framing Focus

Framing helps you to stay focused on how you want to develop your paper. It is a technique in which you will look at your brainstorm and prewriting mapping, listing, or outlining and then block in how you think the paper should develop.

For example, imagine that you want to write a report about the Concorde jet. You have met with members of your peer group and discussed everything you knew about that type of airliner. You have jotted down those ideas and then extended them to a mapping activity (or listing or outlining). Now you are ready to frame.

Framing helps you decide what type of introductory paragraph you want to develop. Review your mapping details and decide which ideas fit into which paragraphs and how many paragraphs you need. Finally, review and determine how you want to conclude your paper.

A framing idea for the Concorde might look like the following example.

introduction	introduction of the subject of the Concorde, explanation of its design, its creators, the features that make it unique, topic sentence stating its superiority
first main body paragraph	discussion about the specifics about the Concorde (this paragraph would report its design and luxury and speed)
second main body paragraph	discussion of its maiden flight, details about its popularity, details about the flight itself, interesting facts about the flight

Framing

Name _____

concluding paragraph

> reworking of superiority idea stating its superior history in aviation, details about how it has changed aviation, broad statement about pioneer aviation and the future

The framing of a paper about the Concorde is not a committed structure, but it is a workable one. At this point you have the information from your mapping or other prewriting technique, and to frame you only need to fill in the boxes with what you think might make a good paper.

Consider your introduction. Ask yourself how to start your paper and then jot down those ideas in the introduction frame.

Next, consider how you want to present your details that you brainstormed and add those to your main body. Keep your ideas together so that they make sense as they become paragraphs. Finally, consider how you will end your paper and fill in the frame for your concluding paragraph.

Once you have finished framing, you have the potential structure needed to develop a full paper. As you develop your rough draft, it may change and that is fine. At least you have a "blueprint" for what you think you want your paper to look like when you are finished writing it.

Directions: Working with one of your topics from the prewriting chapter, fill in the frame for a report. Look carefully at the details you brainstormed and fill in the blocks with the details you think would make an interesting report. Organize the details to match and to develop a flow of ideas. If you do not have enough details for a paragraph, it means that you need to do more research on that topic. Your paper may be a few paragraphs or many, depending on the depth of your detail and the required length of your paper.

introduction

© Instructional Fair • TS Denison

IF19316 Strategies for Writing Success

Framing

Name _____

first main body paragraph   ☐

second main body paragraph   ☐

concluding paragraph   ☐

The previous example illustrates framing for a report. That same structure can be used to frame a narrative writing, a reflective writing, an autobiography, a biography, or a process paper. Basically, details for those types of papers will fit logically into this type of frame. Perhaps the only difference for an autobiography (or a biography) is if you wanted to compare two characters. Then you probably would want to add more paragraphs that offer a pattern and allow for more details.

Because a comparison and/or contrast paper offers a unique pattern for a frame, study the following example.

Comparison and/or contrast papers tend to follow an A-B pattern of development. That may seem like a confusing way to form the frame for that type of paper, but a comparison and/or contrast paper is going to concentrate on two items, people, places, etc., for the theme of the paper. To make things easier to understand, the two items can be labeled A and B.

Framing

For example, if you are going to compare your sister to you, she will be A and you will be B. When you fill out your frame, you can do a paragraph structure that has the following frame pattern:

introduction	introduce the two people being compared, explain the relationship and the history of the two, develop a topic sentence idea that will establish the purpose of the comparison/contrast of the characters
first main body paragraph	This can be a paragraph about only A traits or it can include a split of A and B traits. The base of comparison for this paragraph might be about how the siblings are physically alike and also different.
second main body paragraph	This paragraph may be a full B paragraph to be opposite the previous one if it had been a full A paragraph or it may be an A and B combination comparing and contrasting personality traits. What you choose to place in this paragraph is your choice.
third main body paragraph	This could be another A paragraph with a complete B paragraph following or it could be another A/B split paragraph. If you have a lot of detail to compare or contrast, you will probably want the A/B structure for each paragraph.
another main body paragraph or a concluding paragraph	At this point you may choose to continue to compare details about A and B, depending on how much information you have from your peer discussion and your prewriting mapping, listing, or outlining. A comparison and/or contrast paper can be lengthy. You also may conclude, if you have presented all your material.

Comparison and/or contrast papers are good for discussing two people, places, events, etc. Your framing will help you understand how much detail you have and how many paragraphs you need to do justice to the topic.

Science and social studies topics easily fit this style of paper because they have many details to compare or contrast. Consider this type of structure when making comparisons about scientific phenomena or historical conditions.

Framing

Name _____

Directions: For practice in framing, use prewriting mapping or listing to make a comparison and contrast of a brother or sister, a cousin, a best friend, or someone your age. Once you have your mapping or listing completed, fill in the following frames in preparation for writing a rough draft. This is practice; however, when writing the rough draft, you may choose to use this topic and the details that you place in these paragraph frames. Again, remember that you may change your mind from the framing activity once you begin writing; however, getting a sense of how you think your paper may develop will give you a "blueprint" of its final form.

introduction

first main body paragraph

second main body paragraph

third main body paragraph

fourth main body paragraph

The concluding paragraph would follow this last main body paragraph.

Framing

When writing a persuasive essay, using framing similar to the comparison and/or contrast will help develop a strong paper, one that investigates two sides of an issue.

The creative writing frame is really a matter of choice. You fill it in as your interest and imagination dictate. For example, if you were writing a story about a young girl named Trudi who had a cat named Taffy, you might have a frame like the following.

introduction	This paragraph might introduce Trudi or it might introduce the cat Taffy as she moves from her yard to her house to visit her owner. It might be a full paragraph about the setting or it might have a hint of a future problem. The possibilities are endless since it is a creative writing task.
first main body paragraph	This might be a paragraph that opens with the introduction of the characters who will be involved in the story with Trudi. It might be the first conflict that Trudi experiences. It might be a bit more explanation of Trudi and her friendship with Taffy.
second main body paragraph	This paragraph may be about the plot or the major conflict. It may introduce a new character. It depends on the goal of your story, the whim of your creative direction, and the depth to which you choose to develop this story.
concluding or more main body paragraphs	Your creative writing short story will be as long as you need or desire it to be unless your teacher has decided on a length for your story.

Practice your own frame for creative writing. Consider how you will begin your story, and perhaps fill in your introduction frame box. Then add description, too, to bring your story to life. In each frame after that, decide if you want to add detail, plot, conflict, theme, other characters, etc. It really is up to you to determine what you want to include in a creative writing frame, but what you include will help you develop a good short story.

Framing

Name _____

Decide what your story is about in a brainstorm of mapping or listing and then fill in the frames.

Story plot _____

introduction

first main body paragraph

second main body paragraph

third main body paragraph

You may choose to add more main body paragraphs, depending on your story. You also will need a conclusion frame. Framing will help you develop a good short story.

Framing

Name _____

Rough Draft Construction

Once you develop a frame in this drafting phase of the writing process, you can actually write the rough draft. Remember that the rough draft is just that, rough and unpolished. It is meant to provide room to expand, explore, and investigate how the ideas for the paper will come together. A rough draft allows for mistakes and for decision changes regarding how to develop an idea or expand one. Rough draft construction gives you a place to fully investigate an idea as it becomes a complete composition or paper.

When developing a rough draft, you may want to do a few things that will make your work easier. First, double space so that you have room to make corrections once you proofread the paper but before you write the final draft.

Second, make certain that you refer to your brainstorm and your framing activities. You have taken the time to develop those prewriting steps to be used in the construction of the final paper. It is easy to forget your prewriting work as you become caught up with your paper construction, but you have the "blueprint" to refer to so it is worthwhile to use it.

Third, if you think of a better idea than what you have developed in your brainstorm or framing activity, then try it. It is easy to think that you can only write a paper a certain way, but that is simply not true. If something new, different, or more interesting pops into your head at this point, then add it and be happy that you were able to expand the idea as you constructed your rough draft.

Rough draft construction is a good place to develop ideas and make mistakes. This is not the time to worry about every error or about perfect sentence construction. That will happen later when you do the proofreading and editing part of the writing process. For now, in the rough draft construction section, just enjoy writing your paper and developing your ideas to match the topic of your composition.

To remind yourself of the steps in developing a rough draft, list several of the rules that were just stated above.

1. _____
2. _____
3. _____
4. _____

Framing

Name _____

Rough Draft First Steps

Once you begin to write your rough draft, pay close attention to your framing so that you develop a logical flow of information. Also, maintain your understanding of the purpose of your paper so that you remain focused. If you forget the purpose of the paper, it will be easy to slip off onto a different subject or direction.

While writing the rough draft, it might help to jot down the purpose on a piece of paper and place it near your work area. Some students write the purpose of the paper on a 3" x 5" card and keep that card on the corner of their desk. Each time they write a paragraph, they pick up the card and reread the purpose. Then they read the paragraph they just completed to make certain that the ideas are connected.

Review some of the activities you have used for framing earlier in this chapter and choose two of your favorite framing subjects. Then write the purpose for each framing activity/paper below:

1. _____
2. _____

Choose one of those purposes to work with in developing a rough draft as you complete this section of the writing process. Once you have made your selection, rewrite the purpose on a scrap of paper or a 3" x 5" card and place it at the corner of your desk where you can see it. This is the paper topic and purpose you will work with as you complete the steps of the writing process.

Once you have determined your topic and purpose, it is time to write the rough draft. First, write the introductory paragraph. You may choose to develop a general subject introduction and lead to your topic sentence so it is clear to the reader what you are intending to develop in the complete paper. If you are writing a report, state the topic somewhere in the paper. For example, a report about dinosaurs might have a topic sentence such as "Dinosaurs offer important clues about what our planet experienced that made dinosaurs extinct." If you are writing an autobiography, your topic sentence might be "My experiences made me the person I am today." And if you are writing a persuasive essay, your topic sentence could be like this one: "It is important to remember that hobbies build the ability to commit."

Now look at the subject you selected and the purpose of your paper and write a topic sentence you might want to use in your first paragraph. Write it below:
Topic sentence: _____

Framing

Name _____

Rough Draft—The Whole Package

Your composition will have an introduction that includes the subject of your paper and the topic idea. The introduction is important because it sets the mood and direction for the reader. The reader will understand what you intend to do with your paper by reading your introduction. Maintaining control of your purpose and developing a good topic sentence will help you to state clearly your intent for your paper.

The main body is where you expand and explore your topic. This is the section of the paper where you can explain ideas, expand ideas, and enhance them to make your topic clear to the reader. The main body needs planning and organization before you write so that you stay on task and stay focused.

Remember to look at your framing to maintain the development of your main body. Just as you wrote your purpose on a piece of paper and placed it on your desk to help you stay focused, it is also important to keep your framing handy and refer to it as you write your main body paragraphs. Refer to both the purpose and your framing frequently, and your paper will stay on the topic.

Finally, the concluding paragraph should wrap up what you have been discussing in your paper. Some people like to reword their topic idea and then expand to a general area of the subject. Other writers like to move slowly from the topic idea to a broad area. The concluding paragraph is necessary to avoid simply stopping your paper. You want to conclude and wrap up loose ends. Your paper should have a beginning, a middle, and an ending.

Directions: For practice in organizing your paper, complete the following:
Topic _____
Purpose _____
Main body paragraph ideas (List core ideas for each possible main body paragraph.)
_____
_____
_____
Conclusion _____

This listing of the organization of your paper can be snipped and placed on your desk as you write the rough draft. Once you have completed that task, you will be ready for the next step in the writing process—the rewriting and editing phase. When writing, planning will make the difference between the good paper you are capable of writing and a sloppy paper that does not reflect your writing talent. Organization is the key to a good paper.

Drafting

THE TEACHERS' LOUNGE

This section of the writing process, the drafting section, is really about planning and organizing. Students need to become comfortable with taking the time to consider how to organize. Many times they want just to write the paper without planning. That usually results in a final project that drifts from the subject and is disjointed in detail. If students learn to organize and to plan, they produce papers they are proud of and also avoid frustration. If they avoid frustration, they are eager to try again.

Current Events Jumble—Have students practice the organization of ideas by selecting newspaper articles, laminating them, and then cutting them into blocks that can be mixed up. Students work in teams of up to three students, and you give them an article that has been cut up into several blocks of a few paragraphs per block. Have students read each block and begin to place them in the sequence of the original article. This provides practice in understanding sequence and organization of a written piece.

If you think this is too difficult, then use a school newspaper to start with and work up to the more sophisticated articles from a local newspaper.

Practice Makes Perfect—Develop empty frames that include a block for the introduction, several blocks for the main body, and a block for the conclusion. Students should work together in teams. Once you have read several stories aloud from their textbooks or a classroom book, have them review the story and write the key ideas that match the structure of introduction, main body, and concluding ideas.

Post those completed organization practice sheets on the bulletin board so that they can see the basic structures of different stories they have read.

Great Ideas!—Students have been practicing mapping, listing, outlining, and framing. They are now ready to write a rough draft paper to complete the writing process. It will be to their benefit to have them brainstorm lists of writing ideas for different types of papers so they have options. You can generate interesting topics by having students team and brainstorm topic ideas for reports, persuasive papers, topics of comparison/contrast, biographies, process ideas, and creative story starters and subjects. They will gain practice in peer work, writing in coherent, correct style for display, and they will be able to choose a topic if they are stuck. Collect their ideas and place them in a topic folder. Put it in a convenient place in the room so that students can browse for an idea when they cannot think of one on their own.

CHAPTER SIX
Writing Process
Rewriting/Editing/Publishing

TEACHER INFORMATION

This section assumes that students have worked with the other steps of the writing process. The writing process is sequential, and one step blends with another to create a bridge that will lead to the full development of the paper. The writing strategies of the writing process help students understand that the development of a report, a persuasive paper, a compare and/or contrast paper, an autobiography or biography, a process, or a creative paper is accomplished through specific techniques.

At this point of the writing process, students hopefully have mastered peer discussion of ideas. Also, they should understand the value of prewriting skills that will help them write a good rough draft.

Now they need to understand what to do with their rough draft once it is finished. Rewriting and editing are the natural steps for the rough draft, since it will need polishing.

Once that is finished, students will move to the level of publishing by either reading it aloud or sharing it in some other way.

The writing process offers students the opportunity to express their ideas in a well-written composition or paper. This process is logical and sequential and easily mastered. Students who take the time to learn the writing process are certain to become strong and confident writers.

Peer Editing

Name _____

Editing

Peer editing offers you the chance to have other people help you develop a better paper by inviting your classmates to critique your composition. However, because peer editing tends to be a sensitive activity (having your paper discussed by other members in the class), set up rules and boundaries for peer editing.

There are some common-sense rules, such as not making rude comments about the quality of someone's work. Be polite. When a person on your team reads a paper to the group, the student is placing him or herself in the vulnerable position of being criticized. It is very important to respect the person's efforts and offer constructive criticism, not negative criticism.

Constructive criticism includes offering suggestions for change, but in a way that is positive, not negative. Suggesting that a classmate may need to add more descriptive language is positive, while telling a person that the paper is boring is negative. Suggesting some help with spelling is positive, while saying that the spelling is stupid is negative. When you are part of a peer editing team, respect the feelings of the other members.

Rules for peer editing are very important. In fact, they are so important that it is worth the effort to make up rules for peer editing that can be used by the whole class.

Directions: In a team of up to three students, discuss with your peers what rules should be required for everyone in the class when doing peer editing. Consider things like listening while the person reads his or her paper, asking questions about the details in the paper, knowing how to request more information about the paper's purpose, and adding input about the mechanics or grammar of the paper. What would be the top five rules you feel would keep peer editing positive?

1. _____
2. _____
3. _____
4. _____
5. _____

Once your group has developed its rules, combine them with the rules of other teams and develop the top ten rules for peer editing. Your teacher will make certain that a copy of those rules is posted in the room for all to see and follow. Peer editing is a successful way to learn how to correct mistakes in a paper and how to work with other members in the class.

Polishing for Perfection

Once you have finished writing your rough draft, rewrite and edit your paper. Rewriting means scrutinizing your paper and making corrections if your ideas drifted from your purpose. It is easy to go off task when writing a paper, because new ideas occur to you as you write. Those ideas become interesting and, as you explore them, it is easy to drift from your original purpose or topic. Rewriting gives you the chance to get back on track.

First, discover where you may have left your topic and drifted to a different one. Find the purpose of your paper that you wrote on a piece of scrap paper or a 3" x 5" card and read it again. Think carefully about what it is you intended to write when you scribbled that purpose on the piece of paper.

Now that you remember your purpose for writing, review what you have actually written in your rough draft. As you read each paragraph, check it against your purpose and see if the paragraph and the purpose match. If not, then use a colored pencil to write corrections to bring the paragraph back to the purpose of the paper.

Once you have read your paper for purpose and the compatibility of your paragraphs, proofread your paper. Proofreading involves reading your paper for spelling errors and grammatical errors, including incomplete sentences, run-on sentences, paragraph development problems, verb tense errors, and anything else your teacher has mentioned. Use a colored pencil to circle your errors.

Once you have completed all of the steps that were just discussed, it is time to move to peer editing.

Peer editing means that you will become a part of a team of up to three members. Each person in the team will read his or her paper to the group for help with editing, or correcting the paper. The self-editing you just performed on your paper will help you understand how well-written your paper is and what places may benefit from other people's ideas. Their input and suggestions will help you decide on changes for your paper.

Peer editing has its own rules and boundaries if it is going to be a positive experience. Those rules and boundaries must be respected.

Cleaning up your rough draft in preparation for final draft construction is a necessary part of the writing process. Rather than regarding rewriting as a distasteful task, rewriting should be viewed as an opportunity to make your good composition ideas great, so that you can be proud that the paper you have developed bears your name.

Peer Editing

Polishing and Publishing

The final stage of writing is the polishing and publishing stage. Polishing involves taking the suggestions of your peer editing team and developing a final draft that is free of errors, both in ideas and grammar. Polishing means that the paper will be typed or written by hand in blue or black ink. Polishing takes you through the development of a final draft paper that will demonstrate you did the best you can do. Pay attention to the rules the teacher requires for the paper and follow them carefully.

A polished final draft should be error free and different from the rough draft, if you have made changes according to your purpose and your proofreading. If you find that your final draft is identical to your rough draft, you can be certain that there are errors that need correction. Even the best writers rarely produce a perfect rough draft copy.

A polished final draft should reflect your talent and your ability to complete a task. Take the time to make it a paper that reflects your best efforts. This paper represents you, your thinking, and your effort; it is worth the time to make it a positive reflection.

When completing a final draft of a paper, remember to make changes in ideas, examples, details, description, sentence construction, paragraph development, structure, grammar, and final appearance. Strive to make each paper you compose a well-written paper.

Publishing means that you will now present this polished reflection of yourself to the class. You may have options in the kind of publishing, depending on your teacher and time constraints.

If there is time, you may be expected to read your paper aloud to the class to teach them what you are reporting about, reflecting on, or attempting to prove. If you are asked to read your paper aloud, and you have made your best effort to polish it, then you should have a successful experience with this form of publishing.

If your class is large and it is not possible to read it to the class, then you may be asked to post it in the room for others to read when there is time. Again, this paper will have your name on it, and other students will be able to read what you wrote. If you concentrated on your task, you will have a paper on display that illustrates your talent, your intellect, and your ability to see a task to completion. Consider the image you want to reflect when you are polishing a final draft composition. If you respect your work, and what it means in terms of how you demonstrate your ideas, then make the effort to produce the best paper you can each and every time.

Writing Process
THE TEACHERS' LOUNGE

The writing process is a successful and logical way for students to become strong and confident writers. It is a lengthy process to teach to students, but once they understand the steps in the writing process, it becomes a natural way for them to approach writing. Encouraging them to brainstorm, write, rewrite, edit, and publish are worthy tasks for the time involved. The outcome is worth the effort.

Rubbing Elbows with Greatness—Supplying examples of good writing will give students a chance to observe good writing style. Sometimes it seems that there are not enough hours in the day for students to read on a regular basis. However, taking a few minutes a day to read nonfiction pieces to the class is still a great way to expose them to good writing. Or taking one class period a week for good writing review will expose students to well-written material many times in a semester or a school year.

Finding posters with good ideas about grammar, paragraph development, or punctuation and displaying them on the walls of your classroom help students learn to write better. Encourage students to read the items on display, and they will learn to write better even when sitting in their seats and looking around the room.

A Rule a Day Keeps the Sloppy Writing Skills Away—The beginning of class or the end of class is a good time to teach a grammatical or writing style rule to students. Depending on your preference, you may choose to have them write down the rule each time in a journal or notebook, or you may choose to simply post it on the chalkboard for the day. A rule a day means that in a few weeks students have been exposed to many rules that will help them become better writers.

Positive, Please—Writing is ego-based for most students, so criticism should be positive. When correcting a paper, it is best to follow the "positive comments first, criticism last" rule. Students need to learn the right way to write a paper, but middle school writers are just beginning this exciting exploration. Positive, constructive criticism will probably be most successful in encouraging them to try again or rewrite. The goal of the writing teacher should be to make students successful writers. Positive, constructive criticism seems to be a safe and effective way to accomplish this.